Breaking
the
Speech
Barrier

Breaking the Speech Barrier

Language

Development

Through

Augmented Means

Mary Ann Romski, Ph.D.
Rose A. Sevcik, Ph.D.
Georgia State University
Atlanta

LIBRARY

·P·A·U·L·H·
BROOKES
PUBLISHING C?

Baltimore • London • Toronto • Sydney

Paul H. Brookes Publishing Co.
Post Office Box 10624
Baltimore, Maryland 21285-0624

Typeset by Edington-Rand, Inc., Riverdale, Maryland.
Manufactured in the United States of America by
The Maple Press Company, York, Pennsylvania.

Library of Congress Cataloging-in-Publication Data

Romski, Mary Ann, 1952–
    Breaking the speech barrier : language development through
augmented means / Mary Ann Romski, Rose A. Sevcik.
       p.   cm.
    Includes bibliographical references and index.
    ISBN 1-55766-252-5
    1. Mentally handicapped children—Language—Longitudinal
studies. 2. Mentally handicapped children—Education—Language
arts—Longitudinal studies. 3. Language acquisition—Longitudinal
studies. I. Sevcik, Rose A. II. Title.
    LC4616.R65   1996
    371.92'8—dc20   96-5896
                                                                        CIP

British Library Cataloguing-in-Publication data are available
from the British Library.

Contents

About the Authors

Mary Ann Romski, Ph.D., is Professor of Communication, Psychology and Educational Psychology & Special Education at Georgia State University, Atlanta. She is a certified speech-language pathologist with more than 20 years of clinical experience. A fellow of the American Association of Mental Retardation (AAMR) and the American Speech-Language-Hearing Association (ASHA), her research has focused on language development and intervention for children and youth with mental retardation who do not speak. She has published more than 50 articles on the topic. Dr. Romski is currently chair of the National Joint Committee on the Communication Needs of Individuals with Severe Disabilities, a member of the ASHA Publications Board, Associate Editor for the *American Journal on Mental Retardation,* and Editorial Consultant for *Language, Speech, and Hearing Services in Schools.*

Rose A. Sevcik, Ph.D., is Assistant Research Professor in the Department of Psychology at Georgia State University, Atlanta. Her research has focused on the language and communication development of children and youth with mental retardation and of great apes. Dr. Sevcik has an extensive publication record and has given numerous presentations to national and international audiences. She is a fellow of the American Association on Mental Retardation and currently is the Associate Coordinator for ASHA's Special Interest Division on Augmentative and Alternative Communication. She is also Associate Editor for Language of the *Journal of Speech and Hearing Research* and Consulting Editor for *Augmentative and Alternative Communication* and the *American Journal on Mental Retardation.*

Foreword

The journey to bring communication systems to persons with severe mental retardation is a fascinating one. To one who has been involved in this journey for more than 45 years, the volume at hand represents an extremely important milestone. As an undergraduate in "speech correction" in 1950, one of my primary textbooks cautioned us to avoid clinical attempts to bring speech to "aments." I say this not to denigrate that book's author, but rather to mark the starting point of the journey for many of us in the field of speech-language pathology.

Since that point, the road to bringing communicative power to individuals with serious disabilities has reached many important junctions, and I think it behooves us to look back briefly at some of them. I think such a perusal through this history will help us better understand the major breakthrough that this book represents.

In the 1950s, the perspectives of those who worked in the field of speech-language pathology were firmly fixed on the mechanics of speech production. As we refined methods for phonological reeducation and speech fluency, we heeded the advice of early leaders and, for the most part, focused our clinical efforts primarily on children with the cognitive holdings deemed fully adequate for speech and language development. Children who had not acquired at least some speech and language in typical developmental fashion were considered poor candidates for our efforts.

In the 1960s, however, national attention was beginning to focus on children with mental retardation, and, as clinical researchers and practitioners focused on the mechanics of speech production, we were forced to face our relative ignorance about both the nature and characteristics of the full human *language* system and the nature and characteristics of serious mental retardation.

These two relative voids in our knowledge directed us to travel simultaneously on what for us were two curiously contradictory academic roads. One road followed the behavioral psychology effort to explore the technology of teaching and learning across a wide range of animals and people. The other followed the psycholinguistic effort to understand the structure of the human language system and the means by which it is acquired by children. These two academic pathways were contradictory for theorists and clinicians in speech-language pathology because they were at opposite poles in terms of their view of the potential for teaching better communicative skills to children and youth with severe mental retardation.

The behaviorists of the 1960s and 1970s operated on the premise that one can teach anyone anything, including communicative forms, if appropriate antecedent events and the consequent events (reinforcement) are manipulated in appropriate, systematic ways. Psycholinguists, however, believed that, if the multilayered, complex system that is language is not acquired through the natural language acquisition device that is inherent in the typical child, it is essentially useless to attempt to intervene in the process. Thus, although it was philosophically illogical, clinicians in speech-language pathology and psychology had little choice but to attempt to meld these two disparate knowledge bases and to seek to teach the complex skills of human language structures identified in the psycholinguistic literature through application of the teaching paradigms resulting from the functional analysis of behavior.

Over the ensuing years, the results of these clinical efforts were, in essence, successful failures. Indeed, some speech and nonspeech responses *were* successfully taught to children with severe mental retardation. Such new behaviors, however, rarely became generative in the sense that a basic language was truly learned, continued to grow, and became usable in anything approaching typical social environments. Clearly, something was missing in *both* the behavioral and psycholinguistic models of the times. In retrospect, one can see that it was the same basic element that was missing in each of these theoretical models. The common element was a rather complete misperception of the nature and purpose of human communication. To most psycholinguists, the essence of language was *syntactic structure,* which kept them focused on an abstract model of language as a complex knowledge system that was configured to fit (even exploit) the abilities of the human brain. To behaviorists, the essence of language was its behavioral forms and topographies (i.e., words, phrases, and, finally, syntactic structures), and this viewpoint kept them focused on modeling and reinforcing speech (and nonspeech) behaviors. Although behaviorists *did* recognize that these behavioral forms *referred* to objects and events and were controlled by the contingent behaviors of social partners, they, along with many of the psycholinguists of the day, seem to have missed the fact that all of the behaviors and structures of language were in the service of regulating the stream of interactions inherent in social living. For the most part, each group failed to see that, although these behaviors and systemic structures were critical elements of human language and communication systems, they existed and functioned to give form to social behaviors intended to affect human environments.

When this social-regulatory function of language began to be stressed in the theory and research data of the mid-1970s, clinical teachers finally began to target language forms and structures in terms of their learners' social needs and desires. This perspective resulted in teaching communicative behaviors that could indicate an individual's desire to *interact* with other people rather than to "name" objects and actions; and for children to say such things as, "No, not that, but this," rather than to create a specific syntactic structure such as a verb or noun phrase. Thus, language intervention targets began to be selected in terms of their ability to communicate desired social and interactive functions rather than in terms of their fit with theories of language structure or theories about their precise control by arbitrary training programs of predetermined schedules of antecedent and consequential stimuli. Along with a realization about the importance of social, student-driven communicative repertoires was the companion idea that such repertoires can be best learned in socially interactive contexts in which they are truly useful. Thus, rather than being "trained" in isolated programming sessions, such communicative acts should be "learned by doing" in interactive contexts that are significant for the student and the other people in his or her environment.

This book represents the ultimate of the empirical validation of the choice to enhance language and communication acquisition by choosing to teach socially needed and desired communicative behavior. Furthermore, it demonstrates powerfully that the teaching of this behavior in naturally occurring social contexts is successful with children with severely limiting cognitive disabilities. Beyond this, the teaching research reflected in this volume demonstrates quite convincingly that a combination of symbolic modes that include a computer-driven speech-output device provides the user with functional communication in a variety of contexts.

In short, this book offers the clinician and the theorist alike a data-based validation of current theory regarding the teaching of an empowering communicative repertoire for many children and youth with severe disabilities. One cannot read this book and not be convinced that the use of speech-output devices in socially and educationally relevant milieus is the blueprint for intervention programs for children and youth with severe disabilities. Professionals in many disciplines, as well as individuals with severe disabilities, owe a great debt to these researchers.

James McLean, Ph.D.
Professor Emeritus
University of Kansas
Lawrence

Foreword

The authors have been active in much of the research-to-practice work in the language intervention field. They have helped to develop augmentative communication and other support systems for children who did not have functional communication systems. They also have adapted nonspeech symbol systems to nonspeaking children's daily environments as part of their work to enhance children's educational and social development.

The authors' functional laboratory, bridging research and practice, is virtually unique in the field of language intervention. The early symbol systems and the accompanying procedures that the authors initially used were adapted from an experimental primate laboratory. But beyond these beginning steps, the authors have continued to adapt, analyze, and design procedures to meet the requirements of children and their teachers. The result has been studies that open doors for both instruction and further research. This background is revealed appropriately throughout the book, especially in Part I.

The state of the art in language augmentation is brought out in the various chapters of the book, but especially in Chapter 7, "Integrating Achievements and Outcomes: Access to the World Through the SAL." This chapter explains that the System for Augmenting Language (SAL) provides not only a design for bringing together various components for instruction and support but also a strategy for exchanges among the participating teachers, practitioners, parents, and researchers, which results in further improvements in the system itself. This common focus involving the SAL tends to bring the principal players in the augmented–language learning process into functional relationships. Such functional relationships bode well for continuing progress in the language augmentation field.

This integrative concept and its systematic implementation is state of the art in the field of language development. This book provides the background for this system, as well as the essential data collection and analysis procedures and the assessment of results. As an added bonus, the authors give the reader a good look at this present research, at areas for future research, and even at the expected implementations of their ongoing work.

Richard L. Schiefelbusch, Ph.D.
University Distinguished Professor Emeritus
Schiefelbusch Institute for Life Span Studies
University of Kansas
Lawrence

Acknowledgments

The research described in this book was funded by grant NICHD-06016 to Georgia State University's Language Research Center and, in addition, for a period of time by grant RR-00165 to the Yerkes Regional Primate Research Center, Emory University, Atlanta. Additional support was provided by the Department of Communication and the College of Arts and Sciences, Georgia State University. Across the years of this project, many individuals have contributed to the findings we report.

First and foremost, we are indebted to the youth and their families who participated in our study. Without their continuing cooperation and shared belief in our goals, we would not have been able to report their accomplishments.

The administrative and professional support of the Clayton County, Georgia, schools was essential to the implementation and completion of the study. We thank all the Clayton County teachers, paraprofessionals, speech-language pathologists, physical therapists, and music therapists who have participated in the project since the mid-1980s in so many and varied ways. In particular, we acknowledge the efforts of Dee Dee Baker, Vicki Collier, Nancy Elliott, Kim Hartsell, Maryann Howell, Dottie Jordan, Kent Logan, Dr. Milton McDonald, Dr. James McGarity, Mike Miller, Betty Nelson, Cherry Rayfield, Joan Ross, Teresa Tabor, and Ann Walton-Bowe.

A number of members of the Program Project research team contributed their support to our project. We acknowledge the Director of the Program Project, Duane Rumbaugh, for his foresight in recognizing the applicability of the nonhuman primate work to individuals with severe communication disabilities and for advocating its implementation. We are grateful to the other principal investigators on the Program Project grant, Robin D. Morris and E. Sue Savage-Rumbaugh, for their constant encouragement. As well, we thank Lauren B. Adamson for her unwavering support and creative contributions to our research project. We extend our appreciation to Roger Bakeman for his sound methodological advice and consultation. We acknowledge the apes, Kanzi, Mulika, Sherman, Austin, Lana, Panbanisha, and Panzee for the insights their symbol learning and use have provided about the power of language.

Walt Woltosz of Words+, Steve Gelman of Unicorn Engineering, David Washburn and Ray Taylor of GSU's Language Research Center, and Ben Smith of the Yerkes Center helped us design the "portable" computer-based communication device that our participants initially employed. Greg Turner of Adamlab provided continuing technical support for our participants' use of the WOLF.

Over the years, many undergraduate students, graduate students, and staff have participated in data collection, summary, and analysis. In particular, we thank Joan Baird, Bob Casey, Jocelyn Cassidy, Jody Clay, Kim Deffebach, Greg Kato, Duncan MacArthur, Rhonda McDaniel, Holly Middleton, Erika Minnis, Lynn Nicolaysen, Teresa Plenge, Becky Reumann, Bronwyn Robinson, Byron Robinson, Susan Rodriguez, Connie Russell, Sr. Elaine Sebera, Wendy Sundgren, Alice Taffar, Ruth Watkins, Krista Wilkinson, and Margaret Yebra. We also thank Tawanna Tookes for her able and cheerful administrative assistance. Special thanks to Mary West Rambow for her expertise in phonetic transcription. We extend our appreciation to Andrea Clay for the illustrations that appear in the book.

During a very important time, Jon Miller provided crucial public support of our research effort. We are also grateful to Paul Alberto, Ann P. Kaiser, and Carolyn B. Mervis for their continuing colleagueship.

Finally, Carol R. Hollander provided numerous suggestions and sage advice during the development of the manuscript. We are grateful to her as well for her careful and insightful editing of the volume. Melissa Behm encouraged and guided us throughout this entire project.

To our families. . . .

Breaking
the
Speech
Barrier

Introduction

This book provides a data-based examination of the augmented language development of school-age youth with mental retardation and emphasizes the relationship between research and practice. It is about a project whose a priori aim was to determine whether a speech-output communication device, coupled with naturalistic language intervention, could facilitate the language development of youngsters with moderate or severe mental retardation who did not speak. It is also about the translation of the study's findings into daily educational practice. With a 2-year longitudinal data set from 13 school-age youth, their families, and teachers as its base, the book focuses on how long-term experience with an augmented language system permits an individual to communicate effectively in his educational and social community. In addition, we discuss the intrinsic and extrinsic factors that may have influenced changes in the participants, and, in turn, the system's potential for influencing development. We also present follow-up data on these participants and compare their language and communication skills with two other matched groups of individuals with mental retardation: those who do not speak (who have not experienced this type of intervention) and those who do speak.

We emphasize the critical relationship between research and practice by describing our approach for directly linking the two domains in a public school setting through Project FACTT (Facilitating Augmentative Communication Through Technology). Finally, we conclude by discussing the extension of our research to a new group of children, toddlers with developmental delays who are at significant risk for not developing spoken language. Because of our dual emphasis on research and practice, we are writing for a broad audience of readers that includes researchers, practitioners, and families.

Our philosophy serves to frame how we think about the project and what about the project is important to us. We began with a three-pronged philosophy. First, we believe that individuals with mental retardation are people first. Second, we believe that communication is a basic human right, not a privilege. Third, we believe that research and practice can, and must, work hand-in-hand. If we are to develop long-standing recommended practices, then they must be grounded in empirical, data-based knowledge.

There are several things that this book will not do for the reader. First, it will not provide practitioners with a "cookbook" that explains step-by-step exactly how to teach individuals with severe mental retardation to communicate. Instead, it is designed to share a system, the findings, and the principles that emerged from this system, as well as to share how these principles are being implemented in an educational setting. Second, this book does not address the issue of intervention efficacy. When we began this study, we did not know if the intervention would be successful. Our study was designed to assess the communication outcomes when the System for Augmenting Language (SAL) was employed with individuals who previously had been unsuccessful in learning to communicate. We did not design a study to compare this particular intervention with other interventions. Using a retrospective approach, however, we have examined the resulting outcomes by comparing the participants' skills with other individuals with mental retardation who did not share the same type of experiences.

Our perspective on, and our use of, certain terminology throughout the book deserves some comment as well. First, with respect to gender, the male pronoun is used throughout the book because the participants in this project were all males (see Chapter 3 for discussion). Second, we discuss the language *and* communication development of youth with significant mental retardation because our frame of reference is that language develops for these individuals through the acquisition of functional communication skills. We do not believe that we can easily separate language and communication at these early stages. Third, we refer to our participants as nonspeaking *youth* with moderate or severe mental retardation. For this book, we do not use the term *children*. The individuals who participated in our project had a mean chronological age of 12 years, 3 months, although some were as young as 7 and some were as old as 19 at the initiation of the project. We prefer to use the term *youth* because all participants were school-age, and clearly a few of them were on the verge of young adulthood.

Finally, in Part II of the book, we refer to peer-reviewed journal articles that we published with a number of our colleagues. When we first reference an article, we identify all the authors so that it is clear who contributed to each study.

This book is organized into two major parts. In Part I (Chapters 1 through 4), we provide the reader with the background, a framework, and the tools with which to interpret the findings we present in Part II of the book. Part I of the book includes an orientation to the conceptual framework of the project, information about the foundations of the project, and a characterization of the individuals who participated in this project, as well as a description of the way in which the youth's communicative experiences were structured through the SAL.

In Chapter 1, we provide an introduction to the project by including a conceptual framework in which to view the participants' achievements. Chapter 2 presents an overview of the foundations of the project, emphasizing its roots in animal model research. Chapter 3 characterizes the individuals we studied and focuses on what kinds of communication skills they brought to the task of learning language, as well as on the views that teachers and parents had about them prior to the initiation of the project. Chapter 3 also describes the research aims and design employed. Chapter 4 describes the SAL and discusses the contributions and importance of each of its five components (speech-output communication device, symbols, vocabulary, naturalistic teaching strategies, and resource feedback mechanism). Chapter 4 also introduces the measures, or tools, we employed to develop the language and communication profiles that we report in Part II.

Part II (Chapters 5–9) focuses on the findings from the project, their translation to practice, and future directions for our work. Chapters 5, 6, and 7 present the language, communication and related outcomes, and achievements demonstrated by the individuals who participated in the project. Chapters 5 and 6 focus on the communicative symbol use and vocabulary mastery of the participants. The broader set of extended achievements and outcomes, such as communicative use in community and employment settings, are discussed in Chapter 7. Chapter 8 focuses on the issue of research to practice and characterizes Project FACTT, which is an outgrowth and expansion of the research project. Project FACTT serves to put our research findings into practice in a local public school system. Finally, we conclude in Chapter 9 by examining how we account for our participants' achievements, given their previous histories. We also look forward to the next phase of this ongoing research project by reporting on our research studying toddlers with severe communication disabilities.

PART I

Background, Framework, and Tools

Chapter 1

Developing Language
Through Augmented Means

*If all of my possessions were taken from me, I would choose to keep
the ability to communicate because with it I would win back all the
rest.* (attributed to Daniel Webster)

We begin our book with this dramatic statement because it stresses
the importance of communication to the human enterprise. It is
notable that Webster characterized communication as the one asset
that he would not want to lose, because he could use it to gain back
all his other possessions. This quote underscores what an individual forgoes if he or she never develops adequate functional communication skills.

SIGNIFICANCE OF COMMUNICATION

The significance of communication to human development is never
more striking than in the case of individuals with significant mental
retardation who do not speak. Communication and spoken language skills are of critical importance if an individual is to make
functional gains in all areas of development and, later, to function
successfully in society. From the time children utter their first
words, language is used to meet wants and needs, to maintain
social contact with others, to gain knowledge about the world, and
to exchange information with others (Berko-Gleason, 1988; Berko-
Gleason, Hay, & Cain, 1989; Bruner, 1983). For example, by his
second birthday, Ben, a typically developing toddler, uses utter-

ances such as "Clean Ben off," "Mommy hold me please," and "Call Grandma" to control and manipulate his environment. Given the impact that language can exert on cognitive and social-emotional growth (Rice & Kemper, 1984), there is no question that an impairment in language and communication, especially one of significant magnitude, can affect individuals' development, particularly their cognitive knowledge base and their social interactional skills. Acquiring communication and language skills, then, serves as the key to unlocking the world. For individuals with mental retardation who do not speak, just as for Webster, communication is their most basic and important asset.

This book is about the power communication gives an individual. It describes a project whose goal was to characterize and facilitate the language development process of youth with mental retardation who encountered significant difficulty acquiring spoken language. To open our book, this chapter provides a conceptual and methodological framework in which to place the study of language development through augmented means that is detailed in this volume.

EARLY WORD LEARNING BY
TYPICALLY DEVELOPING CHILDREN

The literature on early language acquisition by typically developing children is a rich one. Language acquisition begins prior to the actual uttering of first words and is evident when children develop an intentional communication repertoire that they use to request and to refer to objects and events in their environments (Adamson, 1995). Such children also have developed some speech comprehension skills, which provide a foundation for their first spoken words (Benedict, 1979; Golinkoff & Hirsh-Pasek, 1990; Oviatt, 1980; Resnick, 1990). The early word learning of typically developing children, then, appears to be couched in their ability to extract relevant information from the linguistic environment and to associate it with their own developing vocal forms in order to express wants and needs (Baldwin & Markman, 1989; Golinkoff, Mervis, & Hirsh-Pasek, 1994; Mervis & Bertrand, 1993). Most children begin talking by gradually building individual vocabularies composed of a range of words (e.g., objects, actions, emotions) (Nelson, 1973) until they evidence a vocabulary growth spurt at about 18–20 months of age (Golinkoff et al., 1994). With this spurt, the rate of vocabulary acquisition increases dramatically, and the children are off on their lifelong journey with language.

LANGUAGE DEVELOPMENT AND MENTAL RETARDATION

Since 1970, research in mental retardation has focused considerable attention on studying the language and communication development of individuals with mental retardation who develop speech, albeit delayed and often incomplete (e.g., Kaiser & Gray, 1993; McLean, Yoder, & Schiefelbusch, 1970; Rosenberg & Abbeduto, 1993; Schiefelbusch & Lloyd, 1974; Warren & Reichle, 1992). The majority of the literature in this area compares the spoken language development of children with mental retardation with that of typically developing children. A small number of studies also have been devoted to investigating intervention strategies (see Rosenberg & Abbeduto, 1993).

In striking contrast to typically developing children and youth with mental retardation who speak are youth with significant mental retardation who encounter serious long-term difficulty in acquiring their first words (Barrett & Diniz, 1989; Beukelman & Mirenda, 1992; Romski & Sevcik, 1988; Schiefelbusch, 1980; Schiefelbusch & Hollis, 1979). In fact, the majority of children and youth with significant mental retardation fail to develop functional spoken words even with considerable speech and language instruction. Anyone who has worked with or studied these individuals can understand the sense of urgency a practitioner is faced with on a daily basis as he or she attempts to serve their needs. Generally speaking, traditional instructional approaches for teaching spoken language have not been successful for this population. Despite the severity of their language impairments, historically, they have been underserved by speech-language pathologists and other professionals. A number of factors have contributed to this, including philosophies that categorically excluded individuals from speech-language intervention, inadequate instructional strategies to meet communication and language needs, lack of supports in the environment, and insufficient professional preparation (National Joint Committee for the Communication Needs of Persons with Severe Disabilities, 1992; Romski & Sevcik, 1988).

Consequently, most of the language teaching efforts for children and youth with significant mental retardation have focused on the immediate clinical or educational goal of developing intervention approaches that permit the youth to communicate basic functional wants and needs. These interventions replaced or augmented individuals' existing receptive and expressive communication skills with, for example, manual signs or visual-graphic symbols (see Mirenda & Iacono, 1990; Romski & Sevcik, 1988, for reviews). Studying language learning through augmented means, as well as the broader educational and social implications of this process, has been a more recent subject of descriptive and empirical examination (Barrett & Diniz, 1989; Bonvillian & Nelson, 1982; Gerber & Kraat, 1992; Romski & Sevcik, 1992) because the clinical or educational needs typically have taken priority.

Specifically, our project was designed to determine how the process of language learning through augmented means develops, the conditions that may best facilitate it, and its broader impact on the course of general development for youth with significant mental retardation. It is such empirical information that can best be translated into recommended practices that, in turn, advance language intervention strategies.

STUDYING AUGMENTED LANGUAGE DEVELOPMENT: SOME CHALLENGES FOR RESEARCHERS

Understanding the process of language acquisition by youth with significant mental retardation who do not speak presents particular challenges for researchers. These challenges include both conceptual and methodological considerations.

Conceptual Considerations

Because the language performance of youth with significant mental retardation who do not speak is hindered by their lack of speech production abilities, we cannot use the course of spoken language development in typically developing children as a model (Gerber & Kraat, 1992; Romski, 1989). Although the study of language development by typically developing children provides some guidance for researchers, we do not know whether youth with significant mental retardation follow a delayed or different course of language development as compared with that of other children. What is needed is a conceptual framework that permits a full consideration of the multiple factors that affect augmented language learning by these youth. We have developed a perspective reflecting a Vygotskian view (Vygotsky, 1978) that emphasizes the contributions and interactions of both intrinsic and extrinsic factors on augmented language learning by youth with significant mental retardation.

First, like typically developing children, these youth bring intrinsic characteristics and skills to the task of learning language. For them, however, their innate abilities have not allowed the process of language learning to unfold via speech. Second, the extrinsic environment plays a critical role in the ability of these youth to learn language through augmented means. For these youth, the conditions under which language is learned, by definition, are altered by the introduction of alternative communication modalities and the teaching strategies employed with them. These conditions modify communicative exchanges in a range of ways. Below, we discuss some of the intrinsic and extrinsic factors that can influence a youth's ability to learn language through augmented means. These factors and their relationships to language learning through augmented means are illustrated in Figure 1.1.

Intrinsic Factors Intrinsic factors are those that the youth brings to the task of learning language through augmented means. These include biological foundations (e.g., neurological status) and psychological competencies (e.g., cognitive skills, communication and language skills, cultural heritage) that influence the expression of the individual's abilities.

From a biological perspective, there are a range of factors that are important to consider. Two such factors are the youth's neurological status and chronological age at the onset of instruction. By definition, youth with significant mental retardation present with diverse neurological profiles (e.g., damage to distinct areas of the brain, active seizure disorders). These differences, which can be difficult to document, may influence the consistency of the youth's ability for language learning. For example, seizure activity could result in a loss of recently acquired skills. The age of the youth at the onset of augmented language experiences is also an important

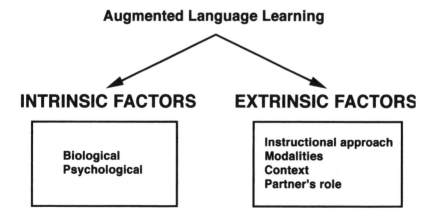

Figure 1.1.   Intrinsic and extrinsic factors that may influence augmented language learning.

factor to consider. School-age youth with significant mental retardation display profiles distinct from those of, for example, very young children. Although the language skills of these youth may appear to be extremely limited, they bring a range of communicative histories and experiences to the task of augmented language learning (Romski & Sevcik, 1992).

Another intrinsic factor to consider is the psychological status of the youth, specifically their language and communication skills. Traditionally, research focused on specifying the *prelinguistic* cognitive abilities of children with severe mental retardation (see Kangas & Lloyd, 1988, for a review). Although their IQs cluster in the severe range of mental retardation, youth who do not learn to speak have varied communication skills and speech comprehension abilities (Baumeister, 1984; Romski & Sevcik, 1988, 1992).

Few studies have characterized the communication skills of children and youth who fail to develop speech (Cirrin & Rowland, 1985; Romski, Sevcik, Reumann, & Pate, 1989). Although none of the participants in these studies had a formal system of communication, they all employed idiosyncratic forms of vocalization, gesture, and physical manipulation to communicate with adults in structured situations as well as in natural environments such as home and school. Because these individuals were able to communicate some simple messages, it appears that the transition to word production and usage was particularly problematic for them.

Early hypotheses suggested that the expressive language impairments of nonspeaking children and youth with mental retardation were the result of motor speech output disorders (Fristoe & Lloyd, 1979). This view assumed that if children and youth were given an alternative output mode, such as manual signs or visual symbols, language learning would proceed at a level consistent with at least their mental age (MA). In turn, it was also assumed that speech comprehension skills would at least approximate MA. Although the performance of a few children and youth is consistent with this view, for most children and youth, speech comprehension skills lag behind MA (Romski & Sevcik, 1988, 1993). Both the literature on the language acquisition of typically developing children and of nonhuman primates provide support for considering the role of speech comprehension skills in language learning. Nelson (1973), for example, proposed that typically developing children who early on produce little speech may rely instead on internally processing the language that they hear in order to advance their linguistic competence. It has also been reported that bonobos (*Pan paniscus*), a species of ape, used speech comprehension as a path for acquiring productive use of visual-graphic symbols (Savage-Rumbaugh, Sevcik, Brakke, Rumbaugh, & Greenfield, 1990).

A youth's ability to use speech comprehension skills as a foundation for augmented language learning may, in turn, rest on two underlying factors: 1) the ability to establish equivalence relationships between spoken words and their referents, and 2) the ability to transfer this information across communication modalities. In the first case, equivalence relationships are those in which the connection between a spoken word and its referent has been established in comprehension during the nonspeaking youth's life experience. In the second case, when an alternative output mode (e.g., visual-graphic symbols) is provided, the equivalence relationships serve as a foundation for the youth to connect the new visual symbols with the already established auditory understandings of spoken words. It is important to note that if individuals have not established equivalence relationships, they may not have a foundation on which to build augmented language skills.

Extrinsic Factors Because nonspeaking youth with mental retardation must learn language through instruction, it is equally important to understand extrinsic factors that contribute to individual variations in learning. Factors extrinsic to the youth are those that make up the language-learning environment or affect that environment. For youth who must learn language through instruction, first and foremost is a consideration of the instructional approach and modalities of instruction used. In addition, specifying the role of communicative partners and the contexts in which communication takes place is essential to understanding the influences on language development through augmented means.

A look at the early literature in the field reveals that the instructional conditions that children with severe mental retardation encountered were variable, at best. Often researchers focused on establishing functional communication skills and did not consider the typical course of language development in their studies of this population (Gerber & Kraat, 1992). Using trial-by-trial instructional strategies, children with severe mental retardation generally acquired situation-specific skills but failed to transfer these to other real-world contexts (Carrier, 1974). More recent studies taught children and youth to use a small number of symbols to request or label items under controlled conditions and then probed transfer to another communicative function (e.g., Keogh & Reichle, 1985; Romski, Sevcik, & Pate, 1988).

One assumption underlying most of these studies was that, without repeated experience in structured environments, the children would not acquire symbol skills (Keogh & Reichle, 1985). A general philosophical shift has occurred, however, that promotes integrating language instruction into naturalistic teaching settings. This shift has reflected the impact of pragmatics (the social use of language in context) in the child language acquisition literature (McLean & Snyder-McLean, 1988; Warren & Kaiser, 1986; Yoder, Kaiser, & Alpert, 1991) and the impact of the generalization of learned language skills to natural environments in the behavioral literature (Warren & Kaiser, 1986; Warren & Rogers-Warren, 1985). Studies with speaking children and with great apes have indicated that language-teaching approaches that highlight the use of language in context may be preferable to those that focus on repetitive drill and practice (Savage-Rumbaugh et al., 1990; Yoder et al., 1991).

Although the use of augmented language devices in natural environments is often recommended (Calculator, 1988), the effectiveness of these procedures for augmented language learning has received little attention to date (Oliver & Halle, 1982). Ultimately, the overall effectiveness of augmented language approaches is measured in terms of an individual's ability to participate in communicative exchanges with various partners in everyday settings. This means that the individual must be both a competent speaker and listener in communicative exchanges. Thus, we began our study with the assumption that a naturalistic teaching method is a viable instructional alternative to structured language intervention approaches for youth with significant mental retardation.

Methodological Considerations

In addition to the conceptual considerations discussed above, there are at least two methodological considerations to be addressed. The first methodological consideration is measurement of the behavioral phenomena. Because spoken language has not been a successful avenue of communicative development for this group of individuals, productive language skills must be established through instruction via another modality (i.e., manual signs or visual-graphic symbols). In some sense, then, the language development of these individuals has been placed solely within the category of intervention outcomes because what is to be measured must be taught before it can be assessed. Initially, a demonstration of the viability of the modality, as well as of the instructional strategy, as a teaching tool is a crucial step in the investigative process of language development with this population. There have been a number of reports of individual positive language outcomes after language instruction through augmented means, such as increased vocabulary size (e.g., Romski et al., 1988) and the production of multisymbol utterances (e.g., Karlan et al., 1982). For example, Reichle and colleagues (Reichle, York, & Sigafoos, 1991) taught individuals to use a generalized requesting procedure. This approach teaches a single consistent symbol, such as "want," which is used in multiple situations to initiate requesting. When a request is initiated, the child is given a choice of items (e.g., cookie, drink). After the child has learned to make generalized requests, differentiated requests for specific referents, such as "want cookie" and "want drink," are incorporated into the child's communicative repertoire. Unfortunately, this type of approach is also the point at which researchers typically end their investigations. An exclusive focus on a specific intervention outcome does not permit an assessment of related language development. If a naturalistic language instructional approach is employed, measurement of the behavioral phenomena must include a broader view of what is both taught and learned.

The second methodological consideration is the research design. Researchers in this field must employ methods that permit them to document and to evaluate precisely how the implementation of an intervention alters the abilities and skills of the participants. Many of the studies conducted to date have been case studies, short-term interventions (i.e., teaching a single skill), or cross-sectional investigations. Because this study focused on a low-incidence population, a cross-sectional, large-group investigation was not feasible, given the number of available subjects. In addition, the process of symbol acquisition and use emerges slowly and cannot easily be captured in a short-term study.

Clearly, longitudinal group research designs and methods offer one approach to studying the process of change following the introduction of augmented language intervention (Gerber & Kraat, 1992; Sevcik & Romski, 1996). Longitudinal designs permit researchers to begin the transition from a reliance on the case study approach to the implementation of a powerful research method for studying groups of individuals over time. Although longitudinal studies are costly endeavors, in terms of both financing and personnel utilization, they provide a powerful and necessary method by which to understand augmented language acquisition and use by youth with significant mental retardation.

Research on augmented language development for youth with significant mental retardation has been focused on the instructional dimensions of teaching individual communicative skills. What has been needed is a characterization of the augmented language learning *process* as well as some considerations of the mechanisms responsible for learning. Thus, as is detailed in this book, our account of this process considers the relative intrinsic influences that the youth brought to the task as well as the extrinsic influences the environment (in the form of the instructional and everyday experiences) exerted on their language development.

REFERENCES

Adamson, L.B. (1995). *Communication development in infancy.* Madison, WI: Brown & Benchmark.

Baldwin, D., & Markman, E. (1989). Establishing word-object relations: A first step. *Child Development, 60,* 381–399.

Barrett, M., & Diniz, F. (1989). Lexical development in mentally handicapped children. In M. Beveridge, G. Conti-Ramsden, & I. Leudar (Eds.), *Language and communication in mentally handicapped people* (pp. 3–32). New York: Chapman & Hall.

Baumeister, A. (1984). Some methodological and conceptual issues in the study of cognitive processes with retarded people. In P. Brooks, R. Sperber, & C. McCauley (Eds.), *Learning and cognition in the mentally retarded* (pp. 1–38). Hillsdale, NJ: Lawrence Erlbaum Associates.

Benedict, H. (1979). Early lexical development: Comprehension and production. *Journal of Child Language, 6,* 183–200.

Berko-Gleason, J. (1988). Language and socialization. In F. Kessel (Ed.), *The development of language and language researchers* (pp. 269–280). Hillsdale, NJ: Lawrence Erlbaum Associates.

Berko-Gleason, J., Hay, D., & Cain, L. (1989). Social and affective determinants of language acquisition. In M. Rice & R.L. Schiefelbusch (Eds.), *The teachability of language* (pp. 171–186). Baltimore: Paul H. Brookes Publishing Co.

Beukelman, D.R., & Mirenda, P. (1992). *Augmentative and alternative communication: Management of severe communication disorders in children and adults.* Baltimore: Paul H. Brookes Publishing Co.

Bonvillian, J.D., & Nelson, K. (1982). Exceptional cases of language acquisition. In K. Nelson (Ed.), *Children's language* (Vol. III, pp. 322–391). Hillsdale, NJ: Lawrence Erlbaum Associates.

Bruner, J. (1983). *Child's talk: Learning to use language.* New York: Norton.

Calculator, S. (1988). Promoting the acquisition and generalization of communication skills by augmented speakers with mental retardation. *Augmentative and Alternative Communication, 4,* 94–103.

Carrier, J. (1974). Nonspeech noun usage training with severely and profoundly retarded children. *Journal of Speech and Hearing Research, 17,* 510–517.

Cirrin, F., & Rowland, C. (1985). Communicative assessment of nonverbal youths with severe/profound mental retardation. *Mental Retardation, 23,* 52–62.

Developing Language / 17

Fristoe, M., & Lloyd, L. (1979). Nonspeech communication. In N.R. Ellis (Ed.), *Handbook of mental deficiency: Psychological theory and research* (pp. 401–430). Hillsdale, NJ: Lawrence Erlbaum Associates.
Gerber, S., & Kraat, A. (1992). Use of a developmental model of language acquisition: Applications to children using AAC systems. *Augmentative and Alternative Communication, 8,* 19–32.
Golinkoff, R., & Hirsh-Pasek, K. (1990). Let the mute speak: What infants can tell us about language acquisition. *Merrill-Palmer Quarterly, 36,* 67–91.
Golinkoff, R., Mervis, C., & Hirsh-Pasek, K. (1994). Early object labels: The case for lexical principles. *Journal of Child Language, 21,* 125–155.
Kaiser, A.P., & Gray, D.B. (Eds.). (1993). *Communication and language intervention series: Vol. 2. Enhancing children's communication: Research foundations for intervention.* Baltimore: Paul H. Brookes Publishing Co.
Kangas, K., & Lloyd, L. (1988). Early cognitive skill prerequisites to augmentative and alternative communication use: What are we waiting for? *Augmentative and Alternative Communication, 4,* 211–221.
Karlan, G.R., Brenn-White, B., Lentz, A., Hodur, P., Egger, D., & Frankoff, D. (1982). Establishing generalized productive verb-noun phrase usage in a manual language system with moderately handicapped children. *Journal of Speech and Hearing Disorders, 47,* 31–42.
Keogh, W., & Reichle, J. (1985). Communication intervention for the "difficult to teach" severely handicapped. In S. Warren & A. Rogers-Warren (Eds.), *Teaching functional language* (pp. 157–194). Baltimore: University Park Press.
McLean, J., & Snyder-McLean, L. (1988). Application of pragmatics to severely mentally retarded children and youth. In R.L. Schiefelbusch & L.L. Lloyd (Eds.), *Language perspectives: Acquisition, retardation, and intervention* (2nd ed., pp. 255–290). Austin, TX: PRO-ED.
McLean, J., Yoder, D., & Schiefelbusch, R.L. (Eds.). (1970). *Language intervention with the retarded.* Baltimore: University Park Press.
Mervis, C., & Bertrand, J. (1993). Acquisition of early object labels: The role of operating principles and input. In A.P. Kaiser & D.B. Gray (Eds.), *Communication and language intervention series: Vol. 2. Enhancing children's communication: Research foundations for intervention* (pp. 287–316). Baltimore: Paul H. Brookes Publishing Co.
Mirenda, P., & Iacono, T. (1990). Communication options for persons with severe and profound disabilities: State of the art and future directions. *Journal of The Association for Persons with Severe Handicaps, 15,* 3–21.
National Joint Committee for the Communication Needs of Persons with Severe Disabilities. (1992). Guidelines for meeting the communication needs of persons with severe disabilities. *Asha, 34*(Supp. 7), 1–8.
Nelson, K. (1973). Structure and strategy in learning to talk. *Monographs of the Society for Research in Child Development, 38*(1–2, Serial No. 139).
Oliver, C., & Halle, J. (1982). Language training in the everyday environment: Teaching functional sign use to a retarded child. *Journal of The Association for Persons with Severe Handicaps, 8,* 50–62.
Oviatt, S.L. (1980). The emerging ability to comprehend language: An experimental approach. *Child Development, 51,* 97–106.

Reichle, J., York, J., & Sigafoos, J. (1991). *Implementing augmentative and alternative communication: Strategies for learners with severe disabilities.* Baltimore: Paul H. Brookes Publishing Co.

Resnick, J.S. (1990). Visual preference as a test of infant word comprehension. *Applied Psycholinguistics, 11,* 145–166.

Rice, M., & Kemper, S. (1984). *Child language and cognition.* Baltimore: University Park Press.

Romski, M.A. (1989). Two decades of ape language research. *Asha, 31,* 81–82.

Romski, M.A., & Sevcik, R.A. (1988). Augmentative and alternative communication systems: Considerations for individuals with severe intellectual disabilities. *Augmentative and Alternative Communication, 4,* 83–93.

Romski, M.A., & Sevcik, R.A. (1992). Augmented language development in children with severe mental retardation. In S.F. Warren & J. Reichle (Eds.), *Communication and language intervention series: Vol. 1. Causes and effects in communication and language intervention* (pp. 131–156). Baltimore: Paul H. Brookes Publishing Co.

Romski, M.A., & Sevcik, R.A. (1993). Language comprehension: Considerations for augmentative and alternative communication. *Augmentative and Alternative Communication, 9,* 281–285.

Romski, M.A., Sevcik, R.A., & Pate, J.L. (1988). The establishment of symbolic communication in persons with severe retardation. *Journal of Speech and Hearing Disorders, 53,* 94–107.

Romski, M.A., Sevcik, R.A., Reumann, R., & Pate, J.L. (1989). Youngsters with moderate or severe retardation and severe spoken language impairments I: Extant communicative patterns. *Journal of Speech and Hearing Disorders, 54,* 366–373.

Rosenberg, S., & Abbeduto, L. (1993). *Language and communication in mental retardation: Development, processes, and intervention.* Hillsdale, NJ: Lawrence Erlbaum Associates.

Savage-Rumbaugh, E.S., Sevcik, R.A., Brakke, K., Rumbaugh, D., & Greenfield, P. (1990). Symbols: Their communicative use, combination, and comprehension by bonobos (*Pan paniscus*). In L. Lipsett & C. Rovee-Collier (Eds.), *Advances in infancy research* (Vol. 6, pp. 221–278). Norwood, NJ: Ablex.

Schiefelbusch, R.L. (Ed.). (1980). *Nonspeech language and communication: Analysis and intervention.* Baltimore: University Park Press.

Schiefelbusch, R.L., & Hollis, J. (Eds.). (1979). *Language intervention from ape to child.* Baltimore: University Park Press.

Schiefelbusch, R.L., & Lloyd, L.L. (Eds.). (1974). *Language perspectives: Acquisition, retardation, and intervention.* Baltimore: University Park Press.

Sevcik, R.A., & Romski, M.A. (1996). *Longitudinal research: Considerations for augmentative and alternative communication.* Manuscript submitted for publication.

Vygotsky, L.S. (1978). *Mind and society: The development of higher psychological processes.* Cambridge, MA: Harvard University Press.

Warren, S., & Kaiser, A. (1986). Incidental language teaching: A critical review. *Journal of Speech and Hearing Disorders, 51,* 291–299.

Warren, S.F., & Reichle, J. (Eds.). (1992). *Communication and language intervention series: Vol. 1. Causes and effects in communication and language intervention.* Baltimore: Paul H. Brookes Publishing Co.

Warren, S., & Rogers-Warren, A. (1985). *Teaching functional language.* Baltimore: University Park Press.

Yoder, P., Kaiser, A., & Alpert, K. (1991). An exploratory study of the interaction between language teaching methods and child characteristics. *Journal of Speech and Hearing Research, 34,* 155–167.

Chapter 2

The Foundations for Our Project

The study described in this book was the third generation of a multigenerational project begun in 1975 by Duane Rumbaugh. The project's roots date back even further, to the early 1970s, when Duane Rumbaugh began the LANA Project at Emory University's Yerkes Regional Primate Research Center and planned to apply his findings to individuals with mental retardation. Within a 5-year period, then, Rumbaugh initiated two independent but inter-related research tracks. The first research track studied the basic requisites to language with great apes as subjects. This work began by studying how the chimpanzee (*Pan troglodytes*) Lana learned to communicate via arbitrary visual-graphic symbols accessed through a computer-linked keyboard developed by Rumbaugh and his colleagues (Rumbaugh, 1977). The second research track studied the language development of children and adults with significant mental retardation who do not speak. This track originated with a feasibility study to determine whether the teaching approach (including the technology, symbol set, and instructional strategies) employed with Lana could be adapted for use by individuals with mental retardation who had not learned to talk (Parkel & Smith, 1979).

ANIMAL MODELS: CONTRIBUTIONS TO LANGUAGE INTERVENTION RESEARCH

Language intervention approaches for youth with mental retardation traditionally focused on translating information from the language acquisition behavior of typically developing children to this population (Bloom & Lahey, 1978; Schiefelbusch & Lloyd, 1974). Although such information about the developmental process provided a general frame in which youth with mental retardation and severe language disabilities could progress, it was frequently difficult to devise discrete instructional procedures for phenomena that occurred spontaneously in the speaking child. For example, what specific skills must be inculcated in a child with severe developmental disabilities in order to produce his or her first words?

In the early 1970s, language interventionists were exploring approaches to teaching language to individuals with mental retardation who did not learn to speak. A number of investigative areas each served as an impetus for initial explorations of nonspeech communication systems with this group of individuals. These included American Sign Language (ASL) with individuals with hearing impairment (Berger, 1970), advances in computer technology for environmental controls (Zangari, Lloyd, & Vicker, 1994), and ape language research (Schiefelbusch & Hollis, 1979).

Although animal models had been employed extensively in biomedical research, they had been little used in psychological research. Perhaps the most prominent behavioral example of the time was the research of Harlow and colleagues at the University of Wisconsin–Madison (e.g., Harlow, Gluck, & Suomi, 1972; Suomi, 1982). They studied atypical behavior in rhesus monkey infants as an animal model for human psychopathology. Language research with great apes served as an animal model for complex communicative behavior because the apes were being taught to use nonspeech communication systems.

Although the typically developing child proceeds rapidly, and somewhat effortlessly, through the initial stages of language acquisition, apes did not. There were questions about whether they could even learn language, given the species-specific nature of the ability as set forth by Chomsky (1965) and others. The findings from ape language research offered an opportunity to better understand some components in the processes of very early language learning. These findings provided a distinct source of information about the development of language and a challenge to intervention researchers and practitioners as they developed and implemented teaching approaches for their subject groups and consumers. A 1976 article in *Asha* (the journal of the American Speech-Language-Hearing Association), for example, was entitled, "If a chimp can learn sign language, surely my nonverbal client can too" (Mayberry, 1976). It was thought that information from language research with apes could enhance our grasp of the difficulties encountered by individuals with significant mental retardation and spoken language impairments.

In 1979, Schiefelbusch and Hollis captured the potential contributions of ape language studies to language intervention research for persons with mental retardation:

> A revolution in thinking about systems of nonspeech language teaching has been precipitated by nonhuman primate research. The chimps have taught us that experimentally viable language models can include alternative symbol sets characterized by flexible receptive and expressive modes, variable task functions, individualized behavioral topographies, and highly specialized pragmatic outcomes. The practical result may be the creation of new strategies and perhaps new models for teaching language to human children. (p. 5)

Only a few projects actually attempted to translate findings from language studies with apes into viable intervention procedures for individuals who did not learn to talk. One example was the work of Carrier (1974) at the University of Kansas. He independently adapted Premack's research with the chimpanzee Sarah (Premack, 1970) and created the Non-Speech Language Initiation Program (Non-SLIP). This program used plastic manipulable symbols to teach sentence structure in a slot-and-filler format. Non-SLIP was employed with individuals with mental retardation who comprehended speech but had difficulty producing it. Porter and Schroeder (1980) reported that 90% of the 31 participants in their Non-SLIP program maintained and generalized the language skills they had learned. McLean and McLean (1974) successfully extended the use of Non-SLIP to two children with autism. They found that the children could use the Non-SLIP symbols to respond to a limited number of social transactions. Although Non-SLIP demonstrated that individuals with mental retardation or autism could learn to structure sentences by using the plastic manipulable symbols, it is no longer used extensively, because it focuses on language structure and does not readily include the use of language in context. In a separate effort, Deich and Hodges (1977) also successfully adapted Premack's work with Sarah in order to teach children with severe mental retardation to communicate.

A few studies translated the sign-language research of the Gardners with the chimpanzee Washoe (e.g., Gardner & Gardner, 1969, 1975) into intervention strategies for children with disabilities. Fouts and colleagues (Fouts, Couch, & O'Neil 1979; Fouts & O'Neil, 1979; Fulwiler & Fouts, 1976) provided an overview of some general adaptations of sign-language instruction with great apes to sign-language teaching efforts for children with autism.

A First Generation of Research with Apes and Humans

At about the same time in the mid-1970s, the first generation of our project was initiated at the Georgia Retardation Center (GRC) in Atlanta. The feasibility study, as it was called, was designed to determine if the computer-linked system, the symbol set, and the instructional methods from the LANA Project might offer a direct human application (Parkel & Smith, 1979; Parkel, White, & Warner, 1977). The goal of the feasibility study was to contribute to the development of language intervention strategies for persons with mental retardation who encountered difficulty in learning to speak, sign, or use other graphic symbol systems.

Lana, a young female chimpanzee, had learned to control her world through sequenced production of visual-graphic symbols, lexigrams, to form stock sentences, such as "PLEASE MACHINE GIVE PIECE-OF APPLE PERIOD" (Rumbaugh, 1977). To produce these symbol strings, Lana used a computer-linked keyboard that objectively captured data and functioned, in principle, as do some now-commercially produced augmentative communication systems. Symbols available for use were dimly illuminated on the keyboard. When selected, the symbols increased in brightness and, at the same time, appeared on projectors above the display in the order of their selection. When confronted with new communicative demands, Lana appropriately modified the component symbols of her sentences and their sequential arrangement to produce novel communications (Pate & Rumbaugh, 1983). Five older children and adolescents who lived in a residential setting learned to communicate via the keyboard system (for detailed discussions see Parkel & Smith, 1979; Romski, White, Millen, & Rumbaugh, 1984). These individuals retained their ability to use symbols more than 18 months after their initial instruction ended (Romski, Sevcik, & Rumbaugh, 1985).

A Second Generation of Research with Apes and Humans

Despite Lana's accomplishments, questions about the precise nature of her individual symbol skills were raised. To address these issues, a second generation of chimpanzees, Sherman and Austin, were taught to communicate by using an instructional procedure that differed notably from that employed in the LANA Project. This research, spearheaded by Sue Savage-Rumbaugh, focused on the expressive acquisition of single symbols rather than stock sentences.

In the discrete trial-training method used, multiple trials of a request-based communicative paradigm were presented in order to establish semantic relationships between symbols and their referents (Savage-Rumbaugh, Rumbaugh, Smith, & Lawson, 1980). For example, the investigator would offer a food item, and the ape's task was to select from the keyboard display the symbol that represented the food. With the correct response, the ape was given the food.

Sherman and Austin also demonstrated that great apes could be taught to employ symbols for inter-individual communication (Savage-Rumbaugh, Rumbaugh, & Boysen, 1978) and that symbolic communication is a complex, long-term process that requires the coordination of many components in order to be successful (Savage-Rumbaugh, Pate, Lawson, Smith, & Rosenbaum, 1983; Savage-Rumbaugh & Sevcik, 1984). For example, Sherman and Austin required receptive-skill training after their productive symbol abilities had been established. Their comprehension was limited to lexigrams alone because they never evidenced comprehension of spoken English words (Savage-Rumbaugh, Sevcik, Rumbaugh, & Rubert, 1985; see also Savage-Rumbaugh, 1986, for a complete description of Sherman's and Austin's accomplishments).

The findings of the initial feasibility study had raised questions about the effects of the language intervention method itself as opposed to the effects of enhanced social experiences alone. The findings also raised questions about whether individuals with severe cognitive disabilities could benefit from such an intervention. To address these questions, a request-based paradigm, adapted from the one employed with Sherman and Austin, was used to establish symbol-referent associations for young adults with severe mental retardation who resided at the Developmental Learning Center (DLC) of the Georgia Regional Hospital, Atlanta. Although initial acquisition was slow, once the relationships between symbols and their referents were established, additional symbol learning occurred rapidly. Symbol comprehension and participant-initiated symbolic communications were some of the results of the production-based instruction (Romski & Sevcik, 1989; Romski, Sevcik, & Pate, 1988). As it was for Sherman and Austin, the learning process for these young adults consisted of the acquisition of component symbol skills (e.g., requesting, labeling, comprehending) that built on one another and resulted in a sophisticated complex of symbol skills. For example, arriving at the study site, one young woman intently rolled her wheelchair to the keyboard, touched a symbol, and went, with a wide grin, to the refrigerator and retrieved the diet cola that she had announced on the keyboard that she wanted. These young adults also exhibited changes in attentional skills and intentional communication skills that were attributable specifically to the language intervention and not simply to increased opportunities for socialization (Abrahamsen, Romski, & Sevcik, 1989).

A Third Generation of Research with Apes and Humans

As we were completing the second generation of work with young adults with mental retardation, a third generation of work with apes was just beginning. Table 2.1 provides an overview of the three generations of ape and human research.

Another species of ape, bonobos or pygmy chimpanzees (*Pan paniscus*), joined the project, and a serendipitous finding emerged. In sharp contrast to Lana, Sherman, and Austin, the young bonobo Kanzi acquired symbols by simply observing the training (which was similar to Sherman's and Austin's) that his adoptive mother, Matata, underwent. At 2½ years of age, Kanzi demonstrated that he had not required explicit instruction in order to learn symbol-referent associations. Given Kanzi's ability to acquire, understand, and use symbols in referential communications without specific training, no discrete trial instructional procedures were adopted or used with him. Investigators modeled symbol use via their communications, both with him and with one another. The receipt of food was not contingent on Kanzi's expressive symbol use. Thus, this instructional approach focused on social-communicative interaction in a seminaturalistic setting using the lexigram symbol system coupled with vocalization and gesture (Savage-Rumbaugh, McDonald, Sevcik, Hopkins, & Rubert, 1986). Kanzi's performance was replicated by his infant sister, Mulika, who also acquired symbols through observation of communicative input and used them flexibly within communicative exchanges (Sevcik, 1989).

Table 2.1. Three generations of the Language Research Center's research with apes and humans

Research generation	Subject group and date of research initiation	
	Ape	Human
First	Lana (1972)	Children and youth in residential setting (1975)
Second	Sherman and Austin (1976)	Young adults in residential setting (1981)
Third	Kanzi (1983)	Youth in home and school settings (1985)

In general, Kanzi's receptive competence exceeded his productive skills. Generally, he demonstrated comprehension of a symbol prior to productive use. Kanzi continued to advance and demonstrated the comprehension not only of single English words but of novel sentences as well (Savage-Rumbaugh, Murphy, Sevcik, Brakke, Williams, & Rumbaugh, 1993). The most striking differences between Kanzi and Sherman and Austin certainly were Kanzi's ability to comprehend spoken words and phrases and his ability to learn to communicate by observing symbol use in naturalistic interactions (Sevcik & Savage-Rumbaugh, 1994).

Not only did Kanzi revolutionize our thinking about what nonhuman primates were capable of, his accomplishments served as an important example of successful symbol learning and use in a natural environment. His achievements blended well with our own plans to shift our focus to younger individuals who had been living at home since birth and were attending public school special education programs. Given our own findings to that point, we concluded that school-age youth who were living at home could make substantial advancements in language and communication development. Thus, we coupled our knowledge about how typical children learn language with what we learned from Kanzi, and we adapted the naturalistic approach to language instruction employed with Kanzi for our study with school-age youth and their communicative partners.

Common Research Components Across Generations

Throughout the generations of research, three commonalities have characterized the ape and human research: 1) the communication system, 2) the instructional methods used to foster functional symbolic communication, and 3) the behavioral measures employed to assess symbol learning (Sevcik, 1993).

An essential aspect of symbolic communication is the use of arbitrary symbols that can stand for, and can take the place of, an object, event, person, or action (Savage-Rumbaugh, Rumbaugh, & Boysen, 1980). The symbol set used in all of the studies we have discussed consists of arbitrary visual-graphic symbols known as lexigrams. Lexigrams are composed of nine geometric forms, or elements, used singly or in combinations of two, three, or four to form symbols (Rumbaugh, 1977). Figure 2.1 shows the nine lexigram elements and examples of some combinations.

Functioning as the equivalents of spoken words, lexigrams were accessed through a computer-linked, touch-sensitive display panel. The display panel, or keyboard, permitted direct selection of

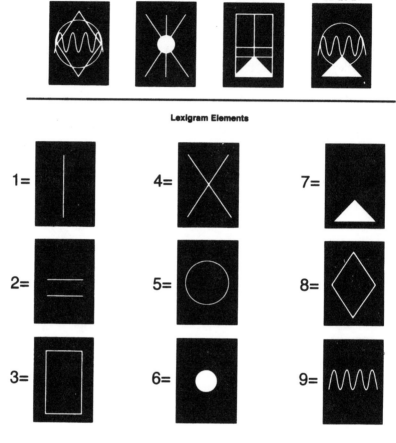

Figure 2.1. The nine lexigram elements and examples of vocabulary items employed in the study.

symbols and provided visual and/or auditory feedback, which has been most recently provided in the form of synthesized speech. (See Chapter 4 for a detailed discussion of how lexigrams were used in our study.)

Across the three generations of research, both discrete trial-training and communicative-modeling strategies were employed to teach language skills. The research methodology moved from highly structured instructional paradigms that taught stock sentences to a focus on comprehension and production of single symbols, to the manipulation of the natural environment in order to foster opportunities for symbolic communication. Two principal types of data sets collected across the generations of longitudinal investigations have characterized the development of symbol acquisition, comprehension, and use. The first data set, derived from on-site contextual judgments of symbol accuracy and pragmatic use, reported on productive and receptive skills in the context of communicative exchanges. The second form of data are receptive and productive vocabulary skill measurements that were administered by the investigators in structured experimental formats. These measurements provide knowledge of specific symbol meanings and relationships apart from the supporting communicative context and with appropriate experimental controls.

A RESEARCH AND PRACTICE MILIEU

The research project described in this book was carried out in two different environments: one focused on research and one centered on practice. The project has been consistently funded by the National Institute of Child Health and Human Development (NICHD). Since 1981, the two research tracks have been housed together following Georgia State University's construction of its Language Research Center (LRC). The LRC, under the direction of Duane Rumbaugh, is an interdisciplinary research center dedicated to the study and enhancement of the linguistic, cognitive, and communicative behaviors of nonhuman and human primates. The center is situated on a 55-acre forested tract about 10 miles from Georgia State University's downtown Atlanta campus. Several buildings are on site and, in addition to providing experimental laboratory space for all the projects, the LRC also houses 12 great apes who participate in a range of behavioral studies about language and cognition. The findings from the LRC's ape language research have obvious implications for the origins of language, as well as for our understanding of the language acquisition process (Romski, 1989). More important, for our purposes, is the contribution of these findings to the study of severe spoken language impairments. Guided by this comparative perspective, findings from our research have permitted us to begin charting the course of initial language development for youth with mental retardation who learn language via instruction. A unique feature of the LRC is that not only is research with nonhuman primates conducted, but also the research findings are actually translated to humans with disabilities (see Romski, 1989; Romski & Savage-Rumbaugh, 1986; Savage-Rumbaugh, Romski, Hopkins, & Sevcik, 1989). Although our project was housed in this research setting, every day we traveled 10–20 miles south to another distinct environment. The homes and classrooms of our participants in Clayton County, Georgia, are the sites where the communicative use and vocabulary assessment data for our study were actually collected. There we were confronted with the everyday realities of the participants in our project and the goals of their parents and educators. The parents' goals were to raise their children. The practitioners' aims were to provide an appropriate education to each individual participant.

Thus, we were surrounded by two distinct environments, each with very different goals and objectives. In order to make the study work, we had to interweave research with recommended practice. The reader will discover, as we did, that this milieu challenged us to conduct sound science in real world settings.

REFERENCES

Abrahamsen, A., Romski, M.A., & Sevcik, R.A. (1989). Concomitants of success in acquiring an augmentative communication system: Changes in attention, communication, and sociability. *American Journal on Mental Retardation, 93*, 475–496.

Berger, S. (1970). A clinical program for developing multimodal language responses with atypical deaf children. In J. McLean, D. Yoder, & R.L. Schiefelbusch (Eds.), *Language intervention with the retarded: Developing strategies* (pp. 212–235). Baltimore: University Park Press.

Bloom, L., & Lahey, M. (1978). *Language development and language disorders.* New York: John Wiley & Sons.

Carrier, J. (1974). Application of functional analysis and a nonspeech response mode to teaching language. In L.V. McReynolds (Ed.), *Developing systematic procedures for training children's language: ASHA Monographs, 18*, 47–96.

Chomsky, N. (1965). *Aspects of the theory of syntax.* Cambridge, MA: MIT Press.

Deich, R., & Hodges, P. (1977). *Language without speech.* New York: Brunner/Mazel.

Fouts, R., Couch, J., & O'Neil, C. (1979). Strategies for primate language training. In R.L. Schiefelbusch & J. Hollis (Eds.), *Language intervention from ape to child* (pp. 295–323). Baltimore: University Park Press.

Fouts, R., & O'Neil, C. (1979). Language intervention in ecological and ethological perspective. In J. Button, T. Lovitt, & T. Rowland (Eds.), *Communication research in learning disabilities and mental retardation* (pp. 249–281). Baltimore: University Park Press.

Fulwiler, R., & Fouts, R. (1976). Acquisition of American Sign Language by a noncommunicating autistic child. *Journal of Autism and Childhood Schizophrenia, 6*, 43–51.

Gardner, R.A., & Gardner, B.T. (1969). Teaching sign language to a chimpanzee. *Science, 165*, 664–672.

Gardner, R.A., & Gardner, B.T. (1975). Early signs of language in child and chimpanzee. *Science, 187*, 752–753.

Harlow, H., Gluck, J., & Suomi, S. (1972). Generalization of behavioral data between nonhuman and human animals. *American Psychologist, 27*, 709–716.

Mayberry, R. (1976). If a chimp can learn sign language, surely my nonverbal client can too. *Asha, 18*, 223–228.

McLean, L., & McLean, J. (1974). A language training program for nonverbal autistic children. *Journal of Speech and Hearing Disorders, 39*, 186–193.

Parkel, D., & Smith, S.T. (1979). Application of computer-assisted language designs. In R.L. Schiefelbusch & J. Hollis (Eds.), *Language intervention from ape to child* (pp. 441–463). Baltimore: University Park Press.

Parkel, D., White, R., & Warner, H. (1977). Implications of the Yerkes technology for mentally retarded human subjects. In D. Rumbaugh (Ed.), *Language learning by a chimpanzee: The LANA Project* (pp. 273–282). New York: Academic Press.

Pate, J.L., & Rumbaugh, D.M. (1983). The language-like behavior of Lana chimpanzee: Is it merely discrimination and paired-associate learning? *Animal Learning and Behavior, 11*, 134–138.

Porter, P., & Schroeder, S. (1980). Generalization and maintenance of skills acquired in Non-Speech Language Initiation Program training. *Applied Research in Mental Retardation, 1*, 71–84.

Premack, D. (1970). Language in chimpanzee? *Science, 712*, 808–822.

Romski, M.A. (1989). Two decades of ape language research. *Asha, 31*, 81–82.

Romski, M.A., & Savage-Rumbaugh, E.S. (1986). Implications for language intervention research: A nonhuman primate model. In E.S. Savage-Rumbaugh, *Ape language: From conditioned response to symbol* (pp. 355–374). New York: Columbia University Press.

Romski, M.A., & Sevcik, R.A. (1989). An analysis of visual-graphic symbol meanings for two nonspeaking adults with severe mental retardation. *Augmentative and Alternative Communication, 5*, 109–114.

Romski, M.A., Sevcik, R.A., & Pate, J.L. (1988). The establishment of symbolic communication in persons with severe retardation. *Journal of Speech and Hearing Disorders, 53*, 94–107.

Romski, M.A., Sevcik, R.A., & Rumbaugh, D.M. (1985). Retention of symbolic communication skills by severely retarded persons. *American Journal of Mental Deficiency, 90*, 441–444.

Romski, M.A., White, R.A., Millen, C.A., & Rumbaugh, D.M. (1984). Effects of computer-keyboard teaching on the symbolic communication of severely retarded persons: Five case studies. *Psychological Record, 34*, 39–54.

Rumbaugh, D.M. (Ed.). (1977). *Language learning by a chimpanzee: The LANA Project*. New York: Academic Press.

Savage-Rumbaugh, E.S. (1986). *Ape language: From conditioned response to symbol.* New York: Columbia University Press.

Savage-Rumbaugh, E.S., McDonald, K., Sevcik, R.A., Hopkins, W.D., & Rubert, E. (1986). Spontaneous symbol acquisition and communicative use by pygmy chimpanzees (*Pan paniscus*). *Journal of Experimental Psychology: General, 115,* 211–235.

Savage-Rumbaugh, E.S., Murphy, J., Sevcik, R.A., Brakke, K., Williams, S., & Rumbaugh, D.M. (1993). Language comprehension in ape and child. *Monographs of the Society for Research in Child Development, 58*(3–4, serial no. 233).

Savage-Rumbaugh, E.S., Pate, J.L., Lawson, J., Smith, S.T., & Rosenbaum, S. (1983). Can a chimpanzee make a statement? *Journal of Experimental Psychology: General, 112,* 457–492.

Savage-Rumbaugh, E.S., Romski, M.A., Hopkins, W.D., & Sevcik, R.A. (1989). Symbol acquisition and use by *Pan troglodytes, Pan paniscus,* and *Homo sapiens.* In P. Heltne & L. Marquardt (Eds.), *Understanding chimpanzees* (pp. 266–295). Cambridge, MA: Harvard University Press.

Savage-Rumbaugh, E.S., Rumbaugh, D., & Boysen, S. (1978). Symbolic communication between two chimpanzees (*Pan troglodytes*). *Science, 201,* 641–644.

Savage-Rumbaugh, E.S., Rumbaugh, D., & Boysen, S. (1980). Do apes use language? *American Scientist, 68,* 49–61.

Savage-Rumbaugh, E.S., Rumbaugh, D., Smith, S.T., & Lawson, J. (1980). Reference: The linguistic essential. *Science, 210,* 922–925.

Savage-Rumbaugh, E.S., & Sevcik, R.A. (1984). Levels of communicative competency in the chimpanzee: Pre-representational and representational. In G. Greenberg & E. Tobach (Eds.), *Behavioral evolution and integrative levels* (pp. 197–219). Hillsdale, NJ: Lawrence Erlbaum Associates.

Savage-Rumbaugh, E.S., Sevcik, R.A., Rumbaugh, D.M., & Rubert, E. (1985). The capacity of animals to acquire language: Do species differences have anything to say to us? *Philosophical Transactions of the Royal Society of London, B308,* 177–185.

Schiefelbusch, R.L., & Hollis, J. (Eds.). (1979). *Language intervention from ape to child.* Baltimore: University Park Press.

Schiefelbusch, R.L., & Lloyd, L. (Eds.). (1974). *Language perspectives: Acquisition, retardation, and intervention.* Baltimore: University Park Press.

Sevcik, R.A. (1989). *A comprehensive analysis of graphic symbol acquisition and use: Evidence from an infant bonobo (Pan paniscus).* Unpublished doctoral dissertation, Georgia State University, Atlanta.

Sevcik, R.A. (1993). Symbolic communication by humans and apes [Abstract]. *Proceedings of the 26th annual Gatlinburg Conference on Research and Theory in Mental Retardation and Developmental Disabilities, 26,* 168.

Sevcik, R.A., & Savage-Rumbaugh, E.S. (1994). Language comprehension and use by great apes. *Language and Communication, 14,* 37–58.

Suomi, S. (1982). Abnormal behavior and animal models of psychopathology. In J. Fobes & J. King (Eds.), *Primate behavior* (pp. 171–215). New York: Academic Press.

Zangari, C., Lloyd, L., & Vicker, B. (1994). Augmentative and alternative communication: An historical perspective. *Augmentative and Alternative Communication, 10,* 27–59.

Chapter 3

Launching the Study

Research Aims,
Participants, and Research Design

In the spring of 1983, a partnership between the Clayton County, Georgia, Public Schools and the Language Research Center (LRC) began when two interested special education teachers and a speech-language pathologist from Clayton County visited the LRC. One teacher had previously visited the LRC as part of a Georgia State University graduate special education class. The three were introduced to the communication research with young adults from the Developmental Learning Center at Georgia Regional Hospital that was ongoing at the time (see Romski, Sevcik, & Pate, 1988), as well as to the LRC's nonhuman primate communication studies (Savage-Rumbaugh, McDonald, Sevcik, Hopkins, & Rubert, 1986). The Clayton County educators observed the young adults using large, semimobile keyboards to communicate with the investigators about foods, objects, and activities in the environment. They also observed Kanzi, the young bonobo, using a keyboard to communicate spontaneously with adult humans in his environment. After a full morning of observations, over lunch we discussed issues related to teaching communication skills to school-age youth. These issues included difficulties in the use of manual signs and picture communication boards, the role of parent involvement, and service delivery models for natural settings.

It was truly a fortuitous meeting! Given our research findings at that point, we were seeking to expand our focus by including in our research younger participants who lived at home as well as settings that offered opportunities for community integration and interaction with typical peers. The special education teachers and speech-language pathologists from Clayton County, in turn, were seeking to incorporate new and innovative instructional strategies into their curriculum. As a result of this meeting, we agreed we would like to work together on a project that used strategies similar to those employed with Kanzi to teach communication to school-age youth. We included this project in our competitive grant renewal, and we obtained the commitment of the Clayton County schools with respect to recruitment of participants and location of the intervention.

During the summer of 1984, the LRC and the Clayton County schools undertook a 6-week cooperative summer program in order to assess the feasibility of the concept and work out the logistics of implementing this type of investigation. This summer program brought 10 children from the Clayton County special education program to the LRC for pilot assessments. Three studies, along with some pilot measures, were completed over the course of the summer program. These studies focused on representational skills (Sevcik & Romski, 1986), symbol discrimination (Meador, Rumbaugh, Tribble, & Thompson, 1984), and symbol processing (Smith, Cash, Barr, & Putney, 1986).

RESEARCH AIMS

In the fall of 1985, with renewed funding from the National Institute of Child Health and Human Development (NICHD), we began the longitudinal study of school-age youth's language and communication development using the System for Augmenting Language (SAL) that is the focus of this book. Our research aims were three-fold: First, we wanted to determine if school-age youth who, to date, had been unsuccessful in learning to communicate could be taught to do so using a naturalistic teaching approach coupled with a speech-output communication device. Second, we wanted to determine if the initial instructional environment would make a difference in their learning. Third, we wanted to determine what language and communication gains, if any, the participants would make over a 2-year period.

Initially, one of the most important tasks in a project such as this is to specify factors intrinsic to the individuals who are participating.

Although "youth with moderate or severe mental retardation" is a commonly used descriptor, grouping individuals by their level of mental retardation provides very little information about their communication profiles beyond the fact that they are highly likely to have significant communication impairments. It was essential that we have detailed descriptions of the youth so that findings from the study could be replicated and any positive outcomes could be translated into practice. In this chapter, we characterize the youth who participated in this study, who they were and were not, and how they were depicted in terms of the field of mental retardation. We describe what kinds of communication skills they brought to the task as well as the perspectives of teachers and parents about them prior to their participation in the research project.

YOUTH WITH MODERATE
OR SEVERE MENTAL RETARDATION

By definition, youth with moderate or severe mental retardation have significant intellectual impairments as evidenced by extremely low scores on intelligence tests (Snell, 1993). Although they are grouped together for diagnostic purposes, they typically exhibit a range of accompanying disabilities that may include, but are not limited to, cerebral palsy, sensory impairments, seizure disorders, other medical conditions, and challenging behavior (Guess & Horner, 1978; Snell, 1993). Such individuals require extensive ongoing support in more than one major life activity in order to participate in their communities and to enjoy a quality of life that is available to individuals with fewer or no disabilities.

Communication Profiles

One area of life activity that more often than not requires support is communication (American Association on Mental Retardation, 1993). The heterogeneous profiles of individuals with mental retardation result in diverse communication profiles. At one end of the continuum are individuals who acquire oral communication skills, albeit slowly and often incompletely, and who exhibit varying degrees of impairment in the comprehension and production of the semantics, syntax, pragmatics, and/or phonology of language (see Rosenberg & Abbeduto, 1993, for a review). At the other end of the continuum are individuals who fail to develop functional spoken communication skills, sometimes even after considerable speech and language instruction directed toward that goal. We were interested in youth at this end of the continuum.

As discussed in Chapter 1, exclusionary criteria, together with a shortage of appropriate output modes and instructional strategies, have limited the communication achievements of these individuals. Since the mid-1980s, changes in educational philosophies and programs, as well as access to assistive technology, have allowed youth with severe disabilities to have greater participatory roles in home, school, community, and work settings. As such increased participation becomes realistically attainable, society's perceptions of this group are slowly but radically undergoing alteration as well.

PARTICIPANTS IN THIS STUDY

Who were the participants in the 2-year study? Thirteen male youth (mean chronological age = 12 years, 3 months; range = 6 years, 2 months–20 years, 5 months) with moderate or severe mental retardation were identified from a pool of about 75 students who were in the Clayton County special education program at the time. Although we did not intentionally exclude females from participation, the individuals who met our criterion (discussed below) and whose parents consented to participate were all males. All participants had resided at home since birth, so immediately this group of participants had distinctly different experiences from the participants in our previous study, who lived in a residential setting. The ethnic composition of the participants was primarily Caucasian; there was one African American participant and one Asian American participant. English was the primary language spoken at home. Although the Asian American family spoke some Chinese at home, they usually did not specifically direct their speech to the participant. All families were of middle to low socioeconomic status.

Participant Selection Process

Prior to the onset of the study, and with the assistance of classroom special education teachers and speech-language pathologists, we identified students in the Clayton County special education program who met a single subject-selection criterion: A potential participant should have a functional vocabulary of no more than 10 spoken-word approximations as determined by a certified school speech-language pathologist's evaluation. Given the chronological age (CA) (mean CA = 12 years, 3 months) of our chosen participants, a vocabulary of 10 spoken-word approximations or fewer suggested that the likelihood of spontaneous development of spoken words certainly had a very low probability at this point in their development.

In addition, all participants were ambulatory and could use direct selection, in the form of a point, to access a communication device. Their individualized education programs (IEPs) documented that each participant had vision and hearing acuity within normal limits.

All of our participants communicated intentionally at the onset of the study. Most of the participants vocalized, albeit unintelligibly, and used some pointing gestures. Some individuals had previous, although unsuccessful, experience with manual signs, Blissymbols, or nonelectronic picture communication boards. A review of IEPs, coupled with the reports of classroom teachers and speech-language pathologists from the 2-year period prior to the initiation of the study, however, indicated that their language and communication development had not changed over the past 2 years.

Initial Descriptive Assessments

We identified our participants across a 2-year period at the end of the 1984–1985 and 1985–1986 school years. Once a participant was identified and parental consent was obtained, we administered a battery of tests to each participant over the summer of 1985 or 1986. The battery of tests permitted us to characterize each individual's cognitive, language, and communication skills prior to implementation of the intervention.

The school system had already categorized each participant in terms of level of mental retardation as defined by Grossman (1983). Level of retardation was assigned as a result of psychological evaluations conducted by certified school psychologists within the past 3 years. These evaluations took into account both IQ, as measured by the Stanford-Binet Intelligence Scale (Terman & Merrill, 1960) and adaptive behavior, as measured by the AAMD Adaptive Behavior Scale (Lambert, Windmiller, Cole, & Figueroa, 1975). Moderate and severe mental retardation were defined by IQs of 50–70 and 20–40, respectively (Grossman, 1983). Three participants (DC, JA, and MH) had a diagnosis of moderate mental retardation, and the remaining 10 participants had a diagnosis of severe mental retardation.

Additional Cognitive Assessments

We administered the Arthur Adaptation of the Leiter International Performance Scale (Arthur, 1952) to gain a standard measure of the participants' nonverbal cognitive skills. The participants' range of nonverbal performance was quite broad—ranging from less than 2 years to 7 years (mean = 3 years, 6 months) with five participants unable to obtain a basal score on the scale. We also administered two scales from the Ordinal Scales of Psychological Development (Uzgiris & Hunt, 1975) to obtain measures of object permanence and means–ends skills. The first scale, the Visual Pursuit and the Permanence of Objects Scale, provided information about the development of the object concept, including the ability to separate objects from actions and the contexts in which they occur. This skill is often associated with the development of words in young, typically developing children (Gopnick & Meltzoff, 1987). The participants all achieved Stage 6 performance on the Object Permanence Scale, the highest stage attainable. The second scale, the Development of Means for Obtaining Desired Environmental Events Scale, measures the development of cause–effect relations, including the ability to show foresight. This skill is often associated with the development of intentional acts (Bruner, 1975). The majority of participants attained Stage 6 performance. Four participants performed at Stage 5, which suggested that they still lacked foresight in novel situations (Uzgiris & Hunt, 1975).

We also included informal measures of matching and sorting ability to ensure that the participants were able to classify objects into categories. The ability to categorize has been related to first language acquisition in typical children (Gopnick & Meltzoff, 1987; Mervis & Bertrand, 1994). On this task, participants had to sort like objects into bins and match objects with other identical objects (e.g., small wooden blocks). All but one participant matched and sorted objects at greater than 98% accuracy (GJ did so with 75% accuracy). Table 3.1 provides this descriptive information about each participant at the project's onset and includes performance on the measures of nonverbal abilities (Leiter International Performance Scale), object permanence, means–ends, and matching and sorting skills.

Finally, we administered an assessment of representational abilities that we had developed (Sevcik & Romski, 1986) to assess identity and nonidentity matching of four stimulus types: objects, photographs, line drawings, and video images (e.g., a small book, its photo, a line drawing of the photo, and a videotaped image of the book). In this assessment, participants matched each type of stimulus to itself (identity) and to every other type of stimulus (nonidentity). Participants' verbal comprehension skills were measured also. As shown in Table 3.2, the majority of the partici-

Table 3.1. Descriptive information about participants at the onset of the study

Participant	Chronological age (years; months)	Medical etiology	Level of retardation	Leiter[a] (years; months)	Matching/ sorting skills (% correct)	Object permanence (Stage)[b]	Means–ends (Stage)[c]
			Home instruction group				
BB	13;5	Cerebral palsy	Severe	3;0	98	6	6
DC	8;9	Unknown	Moderate	5;1	100	6	6
DE	11;11	Down syndrome	Severe	4;0	100	6	6
JL	20;5	Unknown	Severe	<2;0[e]	100	6	6
KH	10;8	Unknown	Severe	<2;0[e]	100	6	5
TF	6;11	Reye syndrome	Severe	<2;0[e]	100	6	5
Mean	12;0			3;0	99	6.0	5.7
			School instruction group				
EC	16;7	Autism	Severe	5;0	100	6	6
FG	20;1	Cerebral palsy	Severe	<2;0[e]	98	6	5
GJ	6;2	Unknown	Severe	<2;0[e]	75	6	6
JA	13;3	Unknown	Moderate	7;0	100	6	6
KW	13;2[d]	Down syndrome	Severe	4;2	100	6	6
MH	7;3	Autism	Moderate	5;0	100	6	6
TE	11;9	Cerebral palsy	Severe	3;3	100	6	5
Mean	12;6			4;1	96	6.0	5.7
Grand mean	12;3			3;6	98	6.0	5.7

[a]Leiter = Arthur Adaptation of the Leiter International Performance Scale (Arthur, 1952).

[b]Object permanence stage ranged from 1 (visual fixation on an object) to 6 (successive invisible displacements of objects) using Scale I (Object Permanence) of the Ordinal Scales of Psychological Development (Uzgiris & Hunt, 1975).

[c]Means–ends stage ranged from 1 (visually attends to objects) to 6 (uses one object as a tool to gain another object) using Scale II (Means–Ends) of the Ordinal Scales of Psychological Development (Uzgiris & Hunt, 1975).

[d]In previous journal reports, KW's chronological age was incorrectly reported as 11;11. This correction changes the mean chronological age reported previously in the journal articles as well.

[e]No basal was achieved, and the participant's age equivalent was estimated to be below the lowest age equivalent available on the test.

pants were successful with these identity and nonidentity representational matching tasks, as well as with the verbal comprehension task. Only FG and GJ encountered any difficulties with the more sophisticated representational matches.

As previously mentioned, the participants' performances on the standardized test, the Leiter, varied greatly. Such variable performance is difficult to interpret and may be the result of

Table 3.2. Assessment of representational abilities

Partici-pant	VC/R	VC/P	VC/L	R/R	P/P	L/L (% correct)	R/P	R/L	R/V	P/L	P/V	L/V
						Home instruction group						
BB	100	100	75	100	100	100	100	100	100	100	100	100
DC	100	100	100	100	100	100	100	100	100	100	100	100
DE	100	100	100	100	100	100	100	100	100	100	100	100
JL	100	100	100	100	100	100	100	100	100	100	100	100
KH	100	100	100	100	100	100	100	100	100	100	100	100
TF	86	100	100	100	100	96	100	100	100	100	100	100
Mean	98	100	96	100	100	99	100	100	100	100	100	100
						School instruction group						
EC	100	100	100	100	100	100	100	100	100	100	100	100
FG	88	50	75	88	81	69	75	56	56	88	75	75
GJ	88	75	100	94	88	75	75	31	50	63	75	75
JA	100	100	100	100	100	100	100	100	100	100	100	100
KW	100	100	100	100	100	100	100	100	100	100	100	100
MH	100	100	100	100	100	100	100	100	100	100	100	100
TE	94	100	100	100	100	100	100	100	94	100	100	100
Mean	96	89	96	97	96	92	93	84	86	93	93	93
Grand mean	97	94	96	99	98	95	96	91	92	96	96	96

VC = Verbal comprehension, R = Real objects, L = Line drawings, P = Photo, V = Video. Four items were assessed in each condition: Book, car, crayon, and telephone.

test-taking demands, such as the type of stimuli or the motor requirements of the task. Their performance on the informal tasks probably better reflected their nonverbal cognitive capacities, because these afforded a more comprehensive look at skills that appear to be germane to language learning. In the main, then, the participants appeared to have many of the nonverbal skills that the child-language literature suggested typically developing children have when they begin to use spoken words as a symbolic form of communication.

Receptive Language and Communication Assessments

Table 3.3 provides information about each participant's receptive language skills prior to the implementation of the intervention. The Peabody Picture Vocabulary Test–Revised (PPVT–R) (Dunn & Dunn, 1981) was employed to measure single-word receptive vo-

Table 3.3. Participants' receptive language profiles at the onset of the study

Partici- pant	PPVT–R[a] (years;months)	ACLC[b]			
		One word	Two words	Three words (% correct)	Four words
Home instruction group					
BB	1;6[c]	65	50	50	40
DC	4;7	96	90	90	70
DE	2;7	78	40	40	30
JL	1;6[c]	80	100	50	60
KH	1;6[c]	50	60	40	40
TF	1;6[c]	50	40	10	30
Mean	2;2	70	63	47	45
School instruction group					
EC	3;1	70	20	30	30
FG	1;6[c]	60	70	30	30
GJ	1;6[c]	34	50	20	20
JA	2;3	94	100	100	50
KW	1;6[c]	86	80	50	60
MH	1;6[c]	88	70	70	60
TE	1;6[c]	80	100	20	30
Mean	1;8	73	70	46	40
Grand mean	2;0	72	67	46	42

[a]PPVT–R = Peabody Picture Vocabulary Test–Revised (Dunn & Dunn, 1981).
[b]ACLC = Assessing Children's Language Comprehension (Foster, Giddan, & Stark, 1983).
[c]No basal was achieved, and the participant's age equivalent was estimated to be below the lowest age equivalent available on the test.

cabulary skills. In this test, from a set of four line drawings (in a two-by-two array), participants are asked to select the correct line drawing as the examiner says, "Show me _____," and announces the target word. Participants' performances ranged from less than 18 months to 55 months, with four participants unable to obtain a basal score (eight consecutive correct responses). To gain a measure of receptive understanding for one-, two-, three-, and four-word combinatorial utterances, we used Assessing Children's Language Comprehension (ACLC) (Foster, Giddan, & Stark, 1983). On this measure, participants are asked to choose the correct black-on-white silhouette when asked, "Show me _____." Single-word vocabulary is first assessed, followed by two-word (e.g., horse standing), three-word (e.g., ball under table), and four-word (e.g., happy little girl jumping) phrases. Our participants' performance consistently deteriorated as the task became increasingly more complex: from a mean of 67% for single-word vocabulary to a mean of 42% for four-word phrases.

Expressive Language Assessments

Table 3.4 shows clearly how little expressive language skill our participants brought to the augmented–language learning task. In order to provide a complete profile of vocal skills, we included measures of vocal and gestural imitation abilities and a rating of

Table 3.4. Participants' expressive language profiles at the onset of the study

Participant	Vocal imitation abilities[a] (Stage)	Gestural imitation abilities[b] (Stage)	Intelligibility Rating Scale (IRS) score[c]	Lexigram matching (% correct)
Home instruction group				
BB	6	6	1.5	100
DC	5	6	2.9	100
DE	6	6	2.2	100
JL	6	6	1.5	100
KH	4	6	1.6	100
TF	5	6	2.0	90
Mean	5.3	6.0	1.9	98
School instruction group				
EC	4	6	1.4	100
FG	4	6	1.0	80
GJ	4	5	1.2	50
JA	4	6	2.3	100
KW	5	4	1.7	100
MH	4	6	3.0	100
TE	6	6	2.6	100
Mean	4.6	5.6	1.9	90
Grand mean	4.9	5.8	1.9	94

[a]Vocal imitation abilities stages ranged from 1 (responsiveness to voice) to 6 (imitation of at least four novel words) using Scale IIIA (Vocal Imitation) of the Ordinal Scales of Psychological Development (Uzgiris & Hunt, 1975).

[b]Gestural imitation abilities stages ranged from 1 (responsiveness to adult gestures) to 6 (imitation of three invisible gestures without objects present) using Scale IIIB (Gestural Imitation) of the Ordinal Scales of Psychological Development (Uzgiris & Hunt, 1975).

[c]Intelligibility Rating Scale (Romski, Plenge, & Sevcik, 1988) ratings ranged from 0 (no response) to 7 (normal intelligibility).

single-word speech intelligibility. In order to determine our participants' abilities to visually discriminate the lexigram symbols they were going to use for communication, we also included a measure of their ability to match identical lexigrams.

In order to assess imitation abilities, we administered Scales IIIA and IIIB of the Ordinal Scales of Psychological Development (Uzgiris & Hunt, 1975), which provide measures of vocal and gestural imitation, respectively. Vocal imitation performance ranged from Stage 4 to Stage 6 (mean = 4.9, Stage 5), indicating that participants could vocally imitate familiar and unfamiliar sound patterns and familiar words, but not at least four novel words. Overall, gestural imitation performance was much better and ranged from Stage 4 to Stage 6 (mean = 5.8, Stage 6) indicating that the participants could imitate familiar invisible (to them) gestures (i.e., sticking out one's tongue), unfamiliar visible and invisible gestures, and complex, delayed motor movements.

In order to gain some standardized indication of the intelligibility of our participants' vocalizations, we obtained audiotaped samples of their vocal responses to photographs of objects prior to the onset of the study. A certified speech-language pathologist naïve to the question of interest rated each sample employing the Intelligibility Rating Scale (IRS) (Romski, Plenge, & Sevcik, 1988) described in Table 3.5. Ratings on the 8-point scale ranged from 0 (no response) to 7 (completely intelligible word). A rating of 1 was defined as a vocal response that was unintelligible and undifferentiated from other vocal responses and was clearly not an attempt to produce the target word. A rating of 2 was defined as an unintelligible vocal response that was differentiated from other responses but was clearly not an attempt to produce the target word. A rating of 3 was defined as a vocal response that was unintelligible, but with at least

Table 3.5. Intelligibility Rating Scale (IRS) (Romski, Plenge, & Sevcik, 1988) for single words

Definition	Rating
Completely intelligible word	7
Intelligible with one articulation error	6
Intelligible with multiple articulation errors	5
"Semi-intelligible" to an experienced listener	4
Unintelligible, but correct syllabification	3
Differentiated vocalization	2
Undifferentiated vocalization	1
No response	0

one phoneme correct, syllabification indicated correctly, or the response clearly recognizable as an attempt at the target word. As Table 3.4 illustrated, the vocal attempts our participants made were not highly intelligible to a naïve listener. Ratings ranged from 1.0 to 3.0 (mean = 1.9) with the majority of participants' mean IRS scores being clustered between ratings of 1 and 2. The vocalizations of only three participants, DC, TE, and MH, were rated higher than 2.5.

In order to determine if the participants could visually discriminate lexigrams from each other, we employed a visual identity matching task. In this task, we asked each participant to match a lexigram to itself when it was presented in a set of three other lexigrams. All but one participant (GJ, with 50% accuracy) did so with greater than 80% accuracy (mean = 94%; range 50%–100%; see Table 3.4). Thus, at the onset of this study, all but one participant easily discriminated the visual-graphic forms from each other. Although GJ's performance was not as accurate as that of the other participants, it was still well above chance, which was 25%.

Finally, we evaluated the adequacy of the structure and function of each participant's physical capability for speech production by conducting an examination of the oral peripheral mechanism. As can be seen in Table 3.6, the participants' oral structures were consistently judged adequate for speech by a certified speech-language pathologist. The functioning of the participants' oral mechanisms, however, was consistently judged to be less than adequate. Specifically, the majority of participants were unable to imitate on command a range of movements of the tongue, lips, and/or the velopharyngeal port mechanism.

General Impressions

The assessment data detailed above provided standard information about each participant's performance and how it compared with the group as a whole. Beyond the data, however, a good diagnostician knows that the complete individual must be considered in the profile (Tomblin, 1994). Our impressions of the participants varied. For example, we were unsure whether TE would be able to learn to communicate using the SAL. When we first met him, he was working by himself in a cardboard cubicle that his teacher and parents had developed in order to focus his attention. He was extremely distractible and had difficulty focusing on visual and auditory input. FG, a young adult in the high school program, had learned to walk only a few summers ago, thanks to the dedication of his father. JA flapped his hands and beat his chest regularly, and DE laughed at almost everything.

Table 3.6. Structure and function of each participant's oral peripheral mechanism, at the onset of the study

Participant	Structure	Function
		Home instruction group
BB	Adequate	Oral structures insufficiently mobile for speech purposes[a]
DC	Adequate	Oral structures insufficiently mobile for speech purposes[a]
DE	Adequate	Adequate
JL	Adequate	Oral structures insufficiently mobile for speech purposes[a]
KH	Adequate	Lack of voluntary control
TF	Adequate	Oral structures insufficiently mobile for speech purposes[a]
		School instruction group
EC	Adequate	Oral structures insufficiently mobile for speech purposes[a]
FG	Adequate	Severe dysarthria
GJ	Adequate	Oral structures insufficiently mobile for speech purposes[a]
JA	Adequate	Apraxia suspected
KW	Adequate	Adequate
MH	Adequate	Oral structures insufficiently mobile for speech purposes[a]
TE	Adequate	Oral structures insufficiently mobile for speech purposes[a]

[a]*Insufficiently mobile* was operationally defined as an inability to imitate on command a range of movements of the tongue, lips, or velopharyngeal port mechanism.

POTENTIAL INFLUENCES ON AUGMENTED LANGUAGE LEARNING

The general impressions and the detailed assessment information we obtained provided a profile of each participant. Although all of the participants were functionally nonspeaking, a number of other characteristics about them varied. Historically, research in the field of augmented language, as in other fields, has grouped together all youth with significant cognitive disabilities who do not speak. Over the years, however, this group has emerged as heterogeneous, and it has been found that individuals bring a broad range of skills to the language-learning task. As our assessment data illustrated, the participants brought a range of intrinsic factors and experience to the augmented–language learning task on which they were about to embark. Their profiles varied depending on the composite of their biological status, their environments, and their experiences. Each individual could, potentially, respond differently to the instructional strategies, which, in turn, would influence the extent to which the participant could profit from the augmented language experience. We identified four specific areas that were likely to influence augmented language learning: medical etiology, cognitive development, and disabilities; communicative experience; speech comprehension skills; and vocal production skills. We now discuss the participants' initial performance in these four areas.

Medical Etiology, Cognitive Development, and Disabilities

Although all of our participants met our subject-selection criteria, the medical etiologies they presented with varied greatly. Three participants had a diagnosis of spastic cerebral palsy, two of the participants had Down syndrome, one had Reye syndrome, and two had autism. The remaining five participants had a disability of unknown etiology.

Regardless of etiology, our participants all exhibited extremely low scores on intelligence tests and adaptive behavior measures, as shown in Table 3.1. In the past, youth with moderate or severe mental retardation were frequently excluded from language instruction because their assessed levels of intelligence and their sensorimotor development were not commensurate with the cognitive and sensorimotor skills that had been linked to early language development (Romski & Sevcik, 1988; Sheehan, Martyn, & Kilburn, 1968). Although one may argue that some basic cognitive skills are essential in order for language to develop, the precise relationship between the domains of cognition and language have not been specified to date (see Rice, 1989; Rice & Kemper, 1984, for reviews). Given the overall impact that language exerts on cognitive development, a lack of productive language skills may put a child at a distinct developmental disadvantage (Rice & Kemper, 1984). Thus, more recently, investigators have argued against excluding youth from language instruction based on intellectual performance or prerequisite sensorimotor skills (Kangas & Lloyd, 1988; Reichle & Karlan, 1985; Romski & Sevcik, 1988). Developing language skills becomes critically important if a youth is to make functional cognitive gains.

Our participants also exhibited a range of related disabilities that could affect their augmented language performance. These included seizure disorders (BB, KH, TF, FG, and TE), challenging behaviors (KH, TF, EC, GJ, and TE), and autistic behaviors (KH, EC, JA, and MH).

Communicative Experience

As an influence, experience is often overlooked in characterizing the factors that may affect augmented language instructional outcomes. Because our participants spoke fewer than 10 productive words, it was presumed that they were functioning at less than a 12- to 18-month-old developmental level, even though chronologically they were well beyond that age (mean CA = 12 years, 3 months; range = 6 years, 2 months–20 years, 5 months). This assumption provided an inaccurate or, perhaps, incomplete description of their competencies, which our assessments indicated. In many respects, our participants functioned beyond the sensorimotor stage of development because they frequently developed and used a range of alternative ways, some idiosyncratic, of communicating with others in familiar environments (Romski, Sevcik, Reumann, & Pate, 1989). For example, JA would take his teacher by the hand and lead her to what he wanted. JL had a vocalization, /əʌu/, which his mother interpreted to mean "I love you." These natural communicative repertoires were obviously employed for prolonged periods of time and included multiple conversational experiences, communicative partners, and settings and did not resemble those of 12- to 18-month-old typical children. Many of our participants had also been through many frustrating years of speech and language therapy directed toward teaching them to talk. They incorporated some of the vocal skills they had learned as part of their communicative repertoires. In general, then, the repertoires were used in more variable contexts and perhaps less flexibly than those of the young, typically developing child.

Speech Comprehension Skills

Although all of the participants had adequate hearing acuity, their ability to process the speech signal also varied considerably. As part of the language profile, we assessed speech comprehension skills, which ranged from little comprehension in context to comprehension comparable with that of a 3- to 4-year-old typical child. The participants who did comprehend speech came to the augmented–language learning task with already established spoken word– referent knowledge (Romski & Sevcik, 1992, 1993; Romski, Sevcik, & Pate, 1988). They understood some verbal commands and knew that words were used to refer to objects, actions, and events in their environments. Their language-learning task, as well as their auditory processing skills, proved to be quite different from those of the participants who did not have such a foundation on which to build augmented language skills. Our research findings suggest that participants who did not understand spoken words out of context had to establish conditional relationships between the visual symbols to be learned and their real-world referents while relying almost exclusively on the visual modality (Romski, Sevcik, & Pate, 1988). As detailed in Chapters 5 and 6, this range of speech comprehension skills turned out to be more important than we initially expected.

Vocal Production Skills

Perhaps one of the most striking observations of an earlier descriptive study with school-age children who were functionally non-speaking (Romski et al., 1989) was the extent to which these children vocalized naturally, though unintelligibly, prior to the implementation of the augmented language experience. Although vocal skills are certainly not necessary for learning an augmented language system, the ability to vocally imitate may play a role in a participant's subsequent gains with speech (Clarke, Remington, & Light, 1986; Romski, Sevcik, Robinson, & Wilkinson, 1990; Yoder & Layton, 1988). As can be seen from Table 3.4, the gestural imitation skills of the participants were better than their vocal imitation skills. Speech intelligibility as measured by the IRS was poor at best.

RESEARCH DESIGN: HOME AND SCHOOL INSTRUCTION GROUPS

Once the participants had been identified and characterized, we divided them into two instructional groups. These two instructional groups were formed based on where the initial instruction was to take place: at home or at school. Participants were paired by chronological age, school placement (i.e., elementary, junior high school, high school), receptive vocabulary skills, and level of mental retardation. Each member of a pair was then randomly assigned to one of the two instructional groups: the home instruction group or the school instruction group. The home member of the seventh pair moved unexpectedly shortly after the initiation of the study and was not able to be replaced. During the first year of the study, the six participants in the home group experienced the intervention only at home, whereas the seven participants in the school group experienced the intervention exclusively at school. During the study's second year, all 13 participants experienced the intervention both at home and at school. The study design is illustrated in Table 3.7.

Communicative Partners

For both the home and school groups, intervention took place in a natural environment for the participant. This design also resulted in the communicative partners differing for each group (parents at home, teachers at school) and thus created, in essence, a second group of subjects in the study. The primary communicative partners all were adults who remained constant across the study. These partners received instruction prior to the study and were monitored during the study (as described in Chapter 4). Participants also had opportunities to interact communicatively with peers with disabilities during their special education classroom activities, as well as with classmates without disabilities during fully integrated activities such as lunchtime at school and with their siblings without disabilities at home (see Chapter 5).

For the home group, the primary communicative partners were parents with at least a junior high school education. There were four two-parent families and two single-parent families (mean CA = 33 years; range = 26–53 years). One parent had completed eighth grade, six of the parents had earned a high school degree, two had attended at least one year of college, and one had a master's degree. For the school group, the primary partners were seven special education teachers who had, at minimum, a bachelor's degree and educational certification in Georgia (mean CA = 27 years; range = 23–33 years).

During the study's second year, all participants used the communication system at home with their parents *and* at school with their teachers. There were now 8 two-parent families, 5 single-parent families (mean CA = 40 years; range = 26–56 years), and 13 teachers (mean CA = 29 years; range = 23–37 years). Table 3.8 lists each participant's primary communicative partner and the partner's age and educational level.

Table 3.7. Study design

Instructional group	Year 1	Year 2
Home instruction group (n = 6)	Home	Home + school
School instruction group (n = 7)	School	School + home

Table 3.8. Profile of each participant's primary communicative partner

Participant	Primary partner	Chronological age (in years)	Educational level
		Home instruction group	
BB	Mother	50	Eighth grade
DC	Mother	34	High school graduate
DE	Mother	33	High school graduate
JL	Mother	52	1 year of college
KH	Father	32	Some college
TF	Mother	27	High school graduate
Mean		38	
		School instruction group	
EC	Teacher	30	B.S.
FG	Teacher	23	B.S.
GJ	Teacher	35	B.S.
JA	Teacher	36	M.Ed.
KW	Teacher	27	M.Ed.
MH	Teacher	31	M.Ed.
TE	Teacher	26	M.Ed.
Mean		26	

Parents and teachers alike were enthusiastic about participating in the study. As the reader will find, they became integral partners in the study. They gave willingly of their time by attending meetings, filling out forms, and participating in regular observations. They share much responsibility for the study's success.

REFERENCES

American Association on Mental Retardation. (1993). *Mental retardation: Definition, classification, and systems of supports* (9th ed.). Washington, DC: Author.

Arthur, G. (1952). *The Arthur Adaptation of the Leiter International Performance Scale.* Chicago: C.H. Steolting.

Bruner, J. (1975). From communication to language: A psychological perspective. *Cognition, 3*, 255–287.

Clarke, S., Remington, B., & Light, P. (1986). The role of referential speech in sign learning by mentally retarded children: A comparison of total communication and sign-alone training. *Journal of Applied Behavior Analysis, 21*, 419–426.

Dunn, L.M., & Dunn, L.M. (1981). *Peabody Picture Vocabulary Test–Revised.* Circle Pines, MN: American Guidance Service.

Foster, R., Giddan, J.J., & Stark, J. (1983). *Assessment of Children's Language Comprehension–1983 Edition*. Palo Alto, CA: Consulting Psychologists Press.

Gopnick, A., & Meltzoff, A. (1987). The development of categorization in the second year and its relation to other cognitive and linguistic developments. *Child Development, 58*, 1523–1531.

Grossman, H. (1983). *Classification in mental retardation*. Washington, DC: American Association on Mental Retardation.

Guess, D., & Horner, R. (1978). The severely and profoundly handicapped. In E.L. Meyen (Ed.), *Exceptional children and youth: An introduction* (pp. 218–268). Denver, CO: Love Publishing Co.

Kangas, K., & Lloyd, L.L. (1988). Early cognitive skill prerequisites to augmentative and alternative communication use: What are we waiting for? *Augmentative and Alternative Communication, 4*, 211–221.

Lambert, N.M., Windmiller, M., Cole, L., & Figueroa, R.A. (1975). Standardization of a public school version of the AAMD Adaptive Behavior Scale. *Mental Retardation, 13*, 3–7.

Meador, D.M., Rumbaugh, D.M., Tribble, M., & Thompson, S. (1984). Facilitating visual discrimination learning of moderately and severely mentally retarded children through illumination of stimuli. *American Journal of Mental Retardation, 89*, 313–316.

Mervis, C., & Bertrand, J. (1994). Acquisition of the novel name-nameless category (N3C) principle. *Child Development, 65*, 1646–1662.

Reichle, J., & Karlan, G. (1985). The selection of an augmentative system in communication intervention: A critique of decision rules. *Journal of The Association for the Severely Handicapped, 10*, 146–156.

Rice, M. (1989). Children's language acquisition. *American Psychologist, 44*, 149–156.

Rice, M., & Kemper, S. (1984). *Child language and cognition*. Baltimore: University Park Press.

Romski, M.A., Plenge, T., & Sevcik, R.A. (1988). *Intelligibility Rating Scale*. Unpublished manuscript.

Romski, M.A., & Sevcik, R.A. (1988). Augmentative communication system acquisition and use: A model for teaching and assessing progress. *NSSLHA Journal, 15*, 61–75.

Romski, M.A., & Sevcik, R.A. (1992). Developing augmented language in children with severe mental retardation. In S.F. Warren & J. Reichle (Eds.), *Communication and language intervention series: Vol. 1. Causes and effects in communication and language intervention* (pp. 113–130). Baltimore: Paul H. Brookes Publishing Co.

Romski, M.A., & Sevcik, R.A. (1993). Language comprehension: Considerations for augmentative and alternative communication. *Augmentative and Alternative Communication, 9*, 281–285.

Romski, M.A., Sevcik, R.A., & Pate, J.L. (1988). The establishment of symbolic communication in persons with severe retardation. *Journal of Speech and Hearing Disorders, 53*, 94–107.

Romski, M.A., Sevcik, R.A., Reumann, R., & Pate, J.L. (1989). Youngsters with moderate or severe retardation and severe spoken language impairments I: Extant communicative patterns. *Journal of Speech and Hearing Disorders, 54*, 366–373.

Romski, M.A., Sevcik, R.A., Robinson, B.F., & Wilkinson, K. (1990, November). *Intelligibility and form changes in the vocalizations of augmented language learners.* Paper presented at the annual meeting of the American Speech-Language-Hearing Association, Seattle, WA.

Rosenberg, S., & Abbeduto, L. (1993). *Language and communication in mental retardation: Development, processes and intervention.* Hillsdale, NJ: Lawrence Erlbaum Associates.

Savage-Rumbaugh, E.S., McDonald, K., Sevcik, R.A., Hopkins, W.D., & Rubert, E. (1986). Spontaneous symbol acquisition and communicative use by pygmy chimpanzees (*Pan paniscus*). *Journal of Experimental Psychology: General, 115,* 211–235.

Sevcik, R.A., & Romski, M.A. (1986). Representational matching skills in persons with severe retardation. *Augmentative and Alternative Communication, 2,* 160–164.

Sheehan, J., Martyn, M., & Kilburn, K. (1968). Speech disorders in retardation. *American Journal of Mental Deficiency, 73,* 251–256.

Smith, S.T., Cash, C., Barr, S., & Putney, R.T. (1986). The nonspeech assessment of hemispheric specialization in retarded children. *Neuropsychologia, 24,* 293–296.

Snell, M. (1993). *Instruction of students with severe disabilities.* Columbus, OH: Merrill/Macmillan.

Terman, L.M., & Merrill, M.A. (1960). *Stanford-Binet Intelligence Scale.* Boston: Houghton Mifflin.

Tomblin, J.B. (1994). Perspectives on diagnosis. In J.B. Tomblin, H.I. Morris, & D.C. Spriestersbach (Eds.), *Diagnosis in speech-language pathology* (pp. 1–28). San Diego, CA: Singular Publishing Group.

Uzgiris, I., & Hunt, J.McV. (1975). *Assessment in infancy: Ordinal scales of psychological development.* Urbana: University of Illinois Press.

Yoder, P., & Layton, T. (1988). Speech following sign language training in autistic children with minimal verbal language. *Journal of Autism and Developmental Disorders, 18,* 217–229.

Chapter 4

The System for Augmenting Language

In order to study the language development of the participants described in Chapter 3, we needed to design an instructional approach for them. This approach had to consider a variety of extrinsic factors in order to provide the communicative supports and experiences that would facilitate a participant's ability to communicate in a conventional manner in everyday environments, including school, home, and community. These supports and experiences became known as the System for Augmenting Language (SAL). We termed our approach a *system* because it consists of organized components that work in concert. One component alone, such as the speech-output communication device itself, is not sufficient. It is the integration of these components that we hypothesize facilitates the language-learning process. Practitioners often report that they find speech-output communication devices on closet shelves not being used. We suspect that this lack of use is because the device was not integrated within an actual total system for communication. Once the system was designed and implementation was begun, we also had to develop tools to measure how the participants were using the SAL and what they were learning about language and communication. In this chapter, we describe the System for Augmenting Language (SAL) and its components, as well as the measurement tools we developed to assess the participants' use of the SAL.

THE FIVE COMPONENTS OF THE SAL

The five components that comprise the SAL are presented in Table 4.1. In this section, we describe each of these components in turn and discuss the contributions that each component makes to the system.

Component 1: Speech-Output Communication Device

This component of the SAL is a microcomputer-based speech-output communication device. Until the early 1980s, the Language Research Center (LRC) developed and produced its own devices for its research efforts. By the time this study began, however, there were a small number of commercially available devices on the market. In addition, it was no longer practical for the LRC to produce, maintain, and repair devices for the expanded number of participants that we expected to have in this project. Over the course of the study, two different commercially available communication devices were employed: the Words+ Portable Voice II (Words+, Inc., 1985) followed by the SuperWOLF (Adamlab, 1988).

The Initial Device When the project was initiated in 1985, the communication device we chose to use was the Words+ Portable Voice II (Words+, Inc., 1985). Although there were other devices available, it appeared to best meet the needs of the project. We wanted a device that was portable, could display symbols at least 1 inch square, and produced synthetic speech that was understandable, a factor that is discussed later in this chapter.

The Words+ Portable Voice II consisted of a specially modified Epson HX-20 notebook computer and an adapted Votrax Personal Speech System voice synthesizer. Included in the portable package were rechargeable power supplies for the Epson and Votrax units and software developed by Words+. Because the participants in this project were unable to read, spell, or write, and

Table 4.1. The five components of the System for Augmenting Language (SAL)

1. Electronic computer-based speech-output communication devices are available for use in natural communicative environments.

2. Appropriate, initially limited symbol vocabularies with the English word printed above each symbol are displayed on the devices.

3. Participants are encouraged, though not required, to use the device during loosely structured naturalistic communicative exchanges.

4. Communicative partners, who have been thoroughly instructed, use the device to augment their speech input to the participants with symbol input.

5. Ongoing resource and feedback mechanisms are provided in order to support the participants and their partners in their communication efforts.

thus could not use the Epson keyboard in a conventional manner, a touch-sensitive Unicorn display panel (Unicorn Engineering, 1985) was added in order to access the Words+ system. The Unicorn display panel measured 14 inches by 21 inches and could accommodate 128 symbols. When a symbol was activated on the Unicorn panel, the Votrax speech-synthesized equivalent of the spoken word for that symbol was produced. We also experimented with an alternative access mode, a Welch-Allen bar code reader, for some of the participants. Here, sweeping a bar code adjacent to the symbol produced the synthetic word. This access mode was quickly abandoned, however, because it proved both difficult and unreliable for our participants to use.

Prior to the implementation of this communication device in school and home settings, it was modified by Words+, Inc., and Unicorn Engineering to meet the specific needs of this group. Words+ software programs were modified extensively, and new software programs were developed at the LRC to operate the Words+ Portable Voice II and its peripherals. These software programs configured the Epson to accept a key press as input, translate the symbolic input into an English word from the stored vocabulary, and send that word to the speech synthesizer as spoken output and to the Epson LED screen as printed output. Additionally, the software programs ensured that accidental key presses would not produce erratic results or halt program execution. The program in the Epson was accessed through a four-choice menu that appeared on the screen. The parents and teachers were able to turn on the program with a single keystroke. This feature permitted the parents and teachers easy access to the system. A specially constructed case protected the Epson unit from liquids and accidental key contact. Although its cover could easily be opened, a latch made access to the keyboard difficult for the participants. These features protected the device from errant activity (e.g., an older sibling reprogramming the Epson, a dog chewing the cable to the Unicorn board). A final set of additions served to optimize portability in the home and school settings. As shown in Figure 4.1, the Words+ unit was positioned on the bottom of a modified luggage cart, and the Unicorn display panel was mounted on the frame of the cart and connected via a cable to the Words+ unit. In order to communicate, a participant touched a symbol on the Unicorn keyboard that, upon release, produced the speech-synthesized word equivalent of the symbol, as shown in Figure 4.2.

Updating the Device In 1988, we replaced the no-longer available Words+ Portable Voice II system with the SuperWOLF

Figure 4.1.   Illustration of the original communication device employed in this study.

Figure 4.2. Participant using the Words+ unit to communicate with a peer. (Illustration by Andrea Clay.)

(Adamlab, 1988). The SuperWOLF weighed a mere 3 pounds (compared to 16 pounds for the Words+ Portable Voice II), was portable, and was one tenth the cost of the initial device. See Figure 4.3 for an illustration of the SuperWOLF.

Two main differences between the Portable Voice II and the SuperWOLF had the potential to affect the participants' abilities to transfer their established skills from one device to the other. First, the ways in which the two devices were accessed were different. As described, to access the Unicorn board, the individual used a touch-and-release action of the appropriate symbol on the display to activate the voice. This required approximately 1.4 seconds. By contrast, the symbol had only to be touched in order to activate the voice on the SuperWOLF, which took approximately 0.7 seconds, or half the time. Second, the way in which the vocabulary was displayed on the two devices was distinctly different. On the Unicorn board, up to 128 one-inch symbols could be displayed simultaneously on two 8-inch by 8-inch panels. On the Super-WOLF, a maximum of 36 one-inch vocabulary items (arrayed on a 6-inch by 6-inch grid) could be accessed at any one time, although up to 378 user-defined vocabulary items were available through 36 individual pages stored in the device.

Figure 4.3.   Illustration of the SuperWOLF.

Even with these differences, all 13 participants in the project readily transferred their extant vocabulary skills from the Unicorn display panel to the SuperWOLF (and subsequently to the Mega-WOLF). On the SuperWOLF, the vocabulary was reorganized by activity so that a single page displayed the vocabulary for one type of activity, for example, leisure activities. We also color-coded each page so that participants who were able to change pages themselves could do so easily. As Chapters 5 and 7 describe, participants were able to continue to expand the size of their vocabularies using the SuperWOLF.

Using Speech-Output Communication Devices: A Rationale Historically, with the exception of a few early studies (Locke & Mirenda, 1988; Romski, Sevcik, & Pate, 1988; Romski, White, Millen, & Rumbaugh, 1984), manual sign systems and, then, cardboard communication boards were the choice for physically typical youth with severe cognitive disabilities. Although a well-established strength of graphic symbols on communication boards for such youth is the use of the visual mode (Fristoe & Lloyd, 1979), this mode requires the partner to both monitor the visual channel and attend to the visual communication produced. We chose to use speech-output communication devices as the medium for language experiences because the voice of a speech-output device would permit the participants to compensate for the use of a visual communication system. Use of a synthetic auditory signal permitted partners to hear the speech feedback produced when a symbol was activated and immediately comprehend the message. This feature is particularly important when individuals are integrated into the general community and interact with unfamiliar communicative partners as we expected our participants would. The speech-output communication device automatically links the individual's visual symbol communication with the familiar spoken modality in social interaction contexts. It permits the youth to use a multimodal form of communication including a voice, albeit artificial, while retaining the visual modality that may be helpful to the youth. Undoubtedly, the addition of speech-output communication devices can permit youth with little or no functional speech to follow a course of language development that is more similar to that of youth who speak because synthetic speech technology empowers them to speak through computerized means.

Once we decided to use devices that produced speech output, we addressed the issue of synthetic speech intelligibility. At the time this study began in 1985, choices of reasonably priced speech synthesizers were limited. The two most readily available speech synthesizers were Echo and Votrax (Beukelman & Mirenda, 1992). The literature on the speech intelligibility of communication device voices was just beginning to be published. Although no synthetic speech system is as intelligible as natural human speech, we viewed the Votrax as a reasonable choice. Toward the end of our previous study, adults with mental retardation were using it successfully to understand the closed set of words it produced. Although studies suggested that the Votrax was among the least intelligible synthesizers (Mirenda & Beukelman, 1987, 1990), these studies did not examine whether intelligibility increased after initial exposure to a closed set of words. Our adult and peer communicative partners reported no difficulty understanding the closed set of words produced by the Votrax system after they had an opportunity to hear the synthetically produced word and pair it with its natural word equivalent. Also, their communicative interactions in context were in accord with their verbal reports regarding the Votrax's speech intelligibility. This finding is consistent with that of Higginbotham, Drazek, and Sussman (1995), who reported that experienced listeners were better able to comprehend discourse produced by synthetic speech than were naïve listeners. Today there are a number of voices to choose from, and digitized speech is also now affordable.

Component 2: Symbols and the Lexicon

The next component of the SAL is the set of visual-graphic symbols and a relevant lexicon. For this project, we employed lexigrams, the arbitrary visual-graphic symbols that were originally developed in the LRC's research with great apes (Rumbaugh, 1977). As described in Chapter 2, lexigrams are composed of nine geometric forms or elements used singly or in combinations of two, three, or four to form symbols (shown in Figure 2.1). In our study, the lexigrams appeared on the display as white element combinations on black backgrounds. Each lexigram is the functional equivalent of a spoken word. We placed the printed English word for each lexigram in reduced size above the symbol in order to facilitate partner interpretation and use (see Figure 4.1).

Our participants began the study with only one symbol displayed, because our research history with adults with severe mental retardation suggested it would be difficult for the participants to learn the conditional relationship between a symbol and its referent. In 1988, we (Romski, Sevcik, & Pate, 1988) reported that two young adults with severe mental retardation, whose instruction took place using a structured trial-by-trial approach within a communicative framework, encountered significant difficulty when a second symbol was added to their display. Their performance dropped, and more than 1,000 trials were required for them to differentiate the first symbol from the second symbol. Given the performance of these two women, we espoused the approach that vocabulary should be constructed through a gradual process that included adding one symbol at a time, providing specific experience with that symbol, and then assessing demonstrated competence prior to the addition of a new symbol.

The initial vocabulary chosen for each participant consisted of 12 referential symbols: four foods, two drinks, and six utensils (e.g., ice cream, chocolate milk, napkin) introduced across a 3-week period. Each participant's vocabulary was individually selected by the investigators in consultation with his parents or teachers and was chosen to meet individual functional communication needs (e.g., requesting) in a mealtime setting. During the first week, one food or drink symbol was available on the display. A second symbol was added after the second week. The participants immediately used the two symbols accurately and consistently, and the remaining 10 symbols were placed on the display after the third week. Their performance was markedly different from that of the young adults described earlier (Romski et al., 1988). The participants learned to differentiate Symbol 1 from Symbol 2 and used them appropriately with comparative ease. Given their performance, we determined that the stepwise strategy of symbol introduction would be too limiting for them. Therefore, for this initial vocabulary expansion, we introduced a group of 10 symbols for a total of 12 symbols in each participant's vocabulary.

When a participant comprehended 8 (66%) of these first 12 lexigrams, 6 additional individually chosen lexigrams, referring to leisure items (e.g., television, radio, magazine, football), were added to the vocabulary for use in leisure settings at home or at school. As participants demonstrated mastery of their vocabulary, and as their partners requested new vocabulary items, 13 social-regulative lexigrams (e.g., please, help), as well as several more referential lexigrams, were added to the vocabulary after the sixth month of the study. Additional vocabulary items were added on an individual basis across the remaining 18 months of the study. Table 4.2 provides a dictionary of the vocabulary for all participants during the study's first 2 years and includes the numbers of the lexigram elements that form the symbol so that readers can re-create the visual forms (using Figure 2.1).

Using Arbitrary Symbols: A Rationale We chose lexigrams as the symbol set for this study for two reasons. First, none of the participants had any experience with them, and thus they all began the study with equivalent symbol-set experience. Second, the purpose of this study was to describe the process of learning to *communicate symbolically.* One critical component of symbolic communication is the use of arbitrary symbols that stand for, and can take the place of, a real object, event, person, action, or relationship (Savage-Rumbaugh, Rumbaugh, & Boysen, 1980). Our past research demonstrated that individuals with severe mental retardation learned from 20 to 75 lexigrams and used them for communication with others (Romski et al., 1988; Romski, Sevcik, & Rumbaugh, 1985; Romski, White, Millen, & Rumbaugh, 1984). More recent studies from another laboratory also indicated that individuals with severe mental retardation can learn to use arbitrary symbols (Brady & McLean, 1996; Brady & Saunders, 1991).

The issue of which symbol set to employ with an individual is a complex and sometimes controversial one that deserves some further discussion (Sevcik, Romski, & Wilkinson, 1991). The main issue of concern is how arbitrary the symbol set is. Symbols that are arbitrary do not resemble the vocabulary item that they represent, whereas nonarbitrary symbols do resemble, to varying degrees, the meanings that they represent. For example, the written word *hat*

Table 4.2. Dictionary of symbol vocabulary for all participants

Referential vocabulary

ball (1+3+4+9)[a]
banana (5+8)
bathroom (4+5)
big wheel (4+5+9)
book (1+7+8)
bowl (2+8+9)
bread (2+5+8)
bucket (3+5+6+7)
cards (1+3)
cereal (7+8)
cheese (2+8)
chocolate milk (1+5+7)
cracker (1+2+6+9)
football (1+5+6+8)
fork (1+6+7+9)
french fries (1+3+4+8)
game (1+2+4+5)
glass (1+2+4+7)
hamburger (6+8+9)
home (2+3+5)
hotdog (1+4+6)
ice cream (3+6+9)
jelly (4+7+8+9)
juice (1+5+9)
ketchup (4+5+8)
knife (5+6+8)
Kool Aid (1+2+5)

macaroni (4+6+8)
magazine (3+5+6)
meat (1+2+5+6)
milk (1+7)
napkin (2+5)
outside (8+9)
pan (1+3+4+5)
paper (1+2+4+9)
peanut butter (3+4+5)
pencil (7)
plate (1+9)
potato chips (2+3+4)
radio (1+2+8)
raisin (1)
record player (2+4+5+9)
records (2+5+7)
salad (2+3+6+7)
school (2+6)
spoon (2+6+7)
straw (1+3+5+8)
swing (2+4+6)
tea (3+6+7)
television (1+2+7+9)
toast (3+8)
tray (1+4+5)
water (5+9)

Social-regulative vocabulary

be quiet (5+7+9)
excuse me (5+6+9)
good (2+9)
goodbye (1+5+7+9)
help (3+5)
hello (1+4+9)
I want (6+7)
I'm finished (2+3+4+5)

I'm sorry (1+3+9)
more (1+4+6+8)
no (6+7+9)
please (1+2+3+7)
stop (6)
thank you (1+2+8+9)
wait (1+3+7+8)
yes (2)

From Adamson, L.B., Romski, M.A., Deffebach, K., & Sevcik, R.A. (1992). Symbol vocabulary and the focus of conversations: Augmenting language development for youth with mental retardation. *Journal of Speech and Hearing Research, 35,* 1333–1344; reprinted by permission.

[a]The numbers in parentheses next to each vocabulary item refer to the nine lexigram elements depicted in Figure 2.1. Using the lexigram elements from Figure 2.1, the lexigram equivalent of the vocabulary item can be created.

is arbitrary and does not resemble the piece of clothing that you wear on your head, whereas the Picture Communication Symbol (PCS) (Johnson, 1981, 1985) for *hat* is a line drawing of the word it represents.

Symbol sets used in research are often different from those used in practice. In research, the purpose of the study often dictates the symbol set employed. For this study, we chose a symbol set that was arbitrary because we wanted to learn about language development. In clinical or educational practice, our experience is that the decision is often a subjective one determined by what the practitioner thinks the individual can use and what symbol set might be easiest for the practitioner to employ. For example, many practitioners choose to employ Picture Communication Symbols (PCSs) (Johnson, 1981, 1985) because they are provided in an organized format and can be displayed easily via a computer software program. In order to guide the practitioner, some methods have been developed to help determine which symbol set(s) to use with an individual (Beukelman & Mirenda, 1992).

Choosing a Lexicon: A Rationale The lexicon available for understanding and expression plays a very important role in learning language through augmented means. The lexicon provides a foundation on which communicative interaction is built. As Yoder and Miller (1972) observed some time ago, "Before the child becomes a language user, he needs to have something to say (a concept), a reason for saying it (semantic intent), and a way to say it (linguistic structure)" (p. 102).

In a more recent conversation, Yoder (D. Yoder, personal communication, July 18, 1995) added two components: a place to say it (a context) and a means to say it (a mode of expression). Clearly, the lexicon in an augmented language system must allow the individual to form messages easily in a variety of contexts.

Although individuals with little or no functional speech are often exposed to a spoken input vocabulary comparable to that of a speaking child, their output is likely to be externally constrained by the number of symbol vocabulary items available on their communication boards. One of the same features that has been proposed to facilitate learning via augmented means, use of recognition rather than recall memory (Fristoe & Lloyd, 1979), may also serve to limit symbol use because of the limited number and type of vocabulary items available at any one time. For this study, we employed the criterion of comprehension of symbols for expanding a participant's vocabulary. We used this criterion because we wanted to ensure that the participants had some understanding of the symbols on the display before we added more symbols to the display.

Referential, easily depictable lexical items have often been chosen for use by youth with mental retardation. The rationale is that referential words are concrete and more easily learned than abstract words. In fact, we began the study with referential symbols for just that reason. Initially, we were hesitant to place nonreferential symbols on the participants' displays. As detailed in Chapter 6, we were pleasantly surprised by the participants' ease of use when we did expand the types of symbols available on their displays.

Component 3: Teaching Through Natural Communicative Exchanges

This component of the SAL is the teaching method. This teaching method included consideration of the location and type of communicative experiences that the participants would have with the speech-output devices. General guidelines on how to manipulate environments so that communication could be facilitated were adapted from the research with bonobos (pygmy chimpanzees) who also communicated via lexigrams on communication devices (Savage-Rumbaugh, McDonald, Sevcik, Hopkins, & Rubert, 1986). Loosely structured naturalistic communicative experiences were provided to encourage, but not require, the participants to use symbols during daily activities. These natural communicative experiences were embedded in the participants' daily routines and activities and promoted contexts for conversational interactions. Such an approach is consistent with contemporary research and theory that recommends the implementation of augmented systems in natural environments in order to 1) emphasize the functional nature of language, 2) facilitate the generalization of communicative routines to diverse contexts, and 3) increase the spontaneity of communicative exchanges (Beukelman & Mirenda, 1992; Calculator, 1988; Romski & Sevcik, 1988a; Warren & Rogers-Warren, 1985). Initially, the location (home or school) in which the exchanges took place was determined by the group in which the participant had been placed. As illustrated in Table 4.3, JL's mother embedded the use of the SAL into the regular afternoon snack routine that she and JL shared on a daily basis.

Rationale for Teaching Through Natural Communicative Exchanges Teaching through natural communicative exchanges may be the most difficult component of the system for some to incorporate, because it is a fairly radical departure from more traditional

Table 4.3. Example of a loosely structured naturalistic communicative exchange

M	And I'm going to use a {KNIFE} to spread it with.
M	J, what would you like for a drink?
M	Tell me what drink you would like.
J	{JUICE}.
M	You would?
M	I kinda thought so.
M	Look what I have at the table.
M	Look here.
=	M holds up the container of orange juice.
M	I already had some {JUICE}.
M	I think I'll shake it.
J	XX.

Transcript is presented in SALT (Systematic Analysis of Language Transcripts, Miller & Chapman, 1985) format, although SALT conventions have been removed for ease of understanding.
{ } = symbol use, == = comment; XX = unintelligible vocalization, M = mother, J = participant.

intervention approaches. Obviously, one basic decision to be made in applied research is where instruction will take place. Although, traditionally, interventions have taken place in isolated settings where the practitioner and youth interact independently, the literature now strongly advocates natural, integrated settings as the preferred environments for communicative instruction (Beukelman & Mirenda, 1992; Calculator, 1988; Romski & Sevcik, 1988a; Warren & Rogers-Warren, 1985). Settings such as the home, school, and community provide familiar locations for the typical occurrence of shared communicative experiences.

Until recently, an overarching theme in the literature has been that youth with severe mental retardation require continuous prompting and structured practice in order to learn language (Reichle, York, & Sigafoos, 1991). However, studies suggest that this may not be the case and support the use of naturalistic teaching strategies. For example, a study of manual sign use by children with mental retardation who did not speak suggested that incidental teaching strategies may function as well as structured teaching approaches (Oliver & Halle, 1982). Yoder, Kaiser, and Alpert (1991) clearly indicated that speaking children acquiring early vocabulary learned better from an incidental teaching approach than from a direct-instruction approach. Research with the bonobo indicates that observational experience with symbols may be superior to drill and practice in promoting arbitrary symbol learning (Savage-Rumbaugh, Sevcik, Brakke, Rumbaugh, &

Greenfield, 1990). Embedding the use of a speech-output device in these everyday settings, then, is a primary component of our teaching approach and brings with it a pair of theoretical assumptions about the nature of the communicative instructional process.

First, communicative symbol use in natural settings implies that communication instruction can be embedded in the ongoing events of everyday life. Opportunities for joint experiences that occur reliably and result in a routine may facilitate the development of communication (Snyder-McLean, Solomonson, McLean, & Sack, 1984). For example, mealtime is often a highly motivating activity for all youth. Embedded in this activity is a sequence of routines or events, such as setting the table, preparing the food, eating and sharing the food, and then cleaning up. Such a sequence of events provides a consistent frame of reference in which communication can occur.

Second, appropriate vocabulary for the participants, as well as for their communicative partners, can be selected for each event in an activity. Once an activity is firmly established, unanticipated variation (e.g., the utensils are absent so the participant cannot begin eating) can be introduced to elicit communication from the youth (e.g., asking for a fork). It may be that during these variations symbol learning actually takes place.

Component 4: Communicative Partner's Use of the Device

The partner's active role in communicative interactions is the next component of the SAL. Because the intervention takes place in natural settings, it is essential that the partner play an active role. This role has two parts: using the system and maintaining the system.

Communicative partners were encouraged to integrate the use of the devices into their own spoken communications by employing what we have characterized as augmented input. In the example, "Tommy, let's go OUTSIDE and ride your BIKE," *outside* and *bike* were symbols touched on the device, produced by the speech synthesizer, and spoken by the partner. This communicative model permitted each family or teacher to incorporate the device's use more easily into individual communicative interactions, as shown in Table 4.4.

To ensure that the primary communicative partners (parents, teachers) understood and were comfortable with their roles, they attended a series of three 1-hour instructional meetings prior to the participant's introduction to the device. These sessions served several functions for the partners. Partners learned about the physical operation of the computer-based communication device,

Table 4.4. Two samples of partner-augmented input

Sample 1

M   Eat your {HOT DOG}.

B   {HOT DOG}.

M   {NAPKIN}.

M   It's on the other side of the plate.

B   XX {points to napkin}.

M   Yeah.

Sample 2

T   Then you get one cracker.

T   One cracker off the plate {PLATE}.

=   In the above utterance, the teacher interrupted herself as she said plate.

P   Plate.

T   Sherrie, do you have {NAPKIN}?

=   P Shows T her napkin.

T   OK.

T   Kevin, what do you want to drink today?

K   XX.

T   OK, bring your {GLASS} and your {PLATE}.

Transcripts are presented in SALT (Miller & Chapman, 1985) format, although SALT conventions have been removed for ease of understanding.

{ } = symbol use; = = comment; XX = unintelligible vocalization; M = mother; T = teacher; K, B = participants; P = peer.

viewed videotapes of interactions with similar devices that illustrated communicative use, and recommended specific vocabulary items to be placed on the Unicorn board to the investigators. During the ongoing intervention, the partners' roles were monitored and continuously reinforced, as is described in the discussion about the next component.

A Rationale for the Partner's Active Role   Because our instruction took place during naturally occurring events in homes, classrooms, and the community, an integral role in the overall instructional process for the participant's adult communicative partners (e.g., teachers, parents) was mandated. Because the SAL focuses on communication in natural settings, a broader concept of participant is fundamental to the instructional process. Partners have two roles in the communication exchange: They are speakers who provide communicative input to the youth, and they are listeners who respond to the youth's communications. By virtue of the visual component, the ways in which the partner communicates with the participant are distinctly different from communications via speech alone. An instructional focus that includes the partners must consider both their speaker and listener roles. Additionally, the partners need instruction in the operation of the device itself.

Partner-augmented input, in turn, serves several functions for the participant. First, it provides a model for how the SAL can be used, in what contexts, and for what purposes. When the SAL is employed as input by the participant's communicative partners, the pairing of the visual symbol with the synthetic speech output may permit the participant to extract previously unobtainable spoken words from the language-learning environment. The specific way in which the symbols are produced and paired with synthetic speech segment the critical word/symbol from the natural stream of speech (e.g., "Let's see your BIKE") and may facilitate the matching of the symbol/word with its physical referent. Second, partner-augmented input has the potential to reinforce the effectiveness of using the system: When a partner incorporates the SAL in successful communicative exchanges, it provides the participant with real-world experiences with the meaning of symbols and the varied functions they serve. The individual then experiences the potential utility and power of the system. Finally, and perhaps most important, partner-augmented input makes an implicit statement to the participant that the SAL provides an acceptable vehicle for communicating, a vehicle that the partner also uses (Romski & Sevcik, 1988a; Sevcik, Romski, Watkins, & Deffebach, 1995).

There are specific practical issues to consider in using an electronic computer-based device. The familiar adult is probably the person who will be responsible for preparing and maintaining the system for regular use. The partner must be comfortable with the mechanical operation of the device (i.e., how to turn it on and off, battery charging); otherwise, he or she will not be able to independently operate the device. The result may be that the device is not employed on a daily basis. There also must be some established mechanism for handling maintenance and repair of the electronic devices, or there may be unnecessary downtime when the communication device is not available for the participant's use.

Component 5: Monitoring Ongoing Use

The final component of the SAL is a resource and feedback mechanism that permitted us to monitor ongoing participant and partner use from the partner's perspective. This resource and feedback mechanism consisted of obtaining systematic information from the participant's primary partner. The research staff then used this information, coupled with the measurement tools that are described in the next section, to gain insights into patterns of communicative use, symbol acquisition accomplishments, and difficulties that were experienced, as well as electronic and technical problems in a particular setting.

To gather this information, we designed the Parent–Teacher Questionnaire (QUEST) (Romski & Sevcik, 1988b), which is shown in Figure 4.4. The QUEST provided a standard format by which to gain an index of the communicative partner's perception of the participant's performance during a specific time period. The investigators collected the information on a regular basis throughout the 2-year study in concert with the Communicative Use Probes, which are discussed below. Later, in Chapters 5 and 6, we present parent and teacher reports taken from the information collected on the QUEST.

In addition to QUEST information, we also held regular meetings with the adult communicative partners during the school year. These meetings provided an opportunity for face-to-face interactions in which to discuss progress and problems.

A Rationale for Monitoring Ongoing Use of the SAL Because the success of the study depended so heavily on the partners' participation and cooperation in everyday settings, it was critical to have a systematic way to monitor the partners' perceptions of the participants' SAL use. This process served to keep everyone on track and address issues regarding SAL use in a timely fashion. For example, after about 3 months of SAL use, parents and teachers, during our meetings and on the QUEST, requested that the participants' lexicons be expanded to include social-regulative symbols. This type of addition to the lexicon was not something we had originally planned to include in the early phases of the study. We realized, however, that if the parents and teachers were going to continue working with us, we needed to respond to their requests. We did, and the addition of social-regulative symbols facilitated the communicative interactions in unexpected ways, as described in Chapters 5 and 6.

METHODS OF MEASURING THE INFLUENCE OF THE SAL

This section presents an overview of the two main assessment measures, Communicative Use Probes (CUPs) and Vocabulary Assessment Measures (VAMs), that served as the databases for the development of a comprehensive profile of the participants' augmented language learning and use over time. Because the SAL was used in everyday settings and communicative partners essentially

Parent–Teacher Questionnaire

Date: _____ Probe #: _____

Parent/Teacher: _____

Participant: _____

Interviewer: _____

Please place a checkmark (✓) next to the response(s) that best describe(s) your experience during the past month.

1. How frequently did _____ use the symbols/communicative system this past month?

   Daily, 5–7 days _____

   Sometimes, 1–4 days _____

   Not at all, 0 days _____

2. When did _____ use the symbols/communicative system this past month?

   During mealtime _____   Which one? _____

   During snack time _____

   During home living class _____

   During leisure time _____

   Other _____

3. What symbols did _____ most frequently use?

   Please list: _____

   _____

4. Has he learned or used new symbols this month?

   Yes _____   No _____

   Please describe: _____

   _____

4a. When _____ used the system, did he use only one symbol at a time? _____

   More than one symbol at a time? _____

   A combination of both of the above? _____

4b. When _____ used more than one symbol at a time, how many symbols did he put together? _____

   Please give examples: _____

5. Did _____ initiate any symbol communications with you this month?

   Yes _____   No _____   If so, how did he gain your attention?

   By the symbol alone _____

   By a vocalization _____

   By a gesture _____

Figure 4.4. Parent–Teacher Questionnaire (QUEST). (From Romski, M.A., & Sevcik, R.A. [1988b]. Augmentative communication system acquisition and use: A model for teaching and assessing progress. *NSSLHA Journal, 15,* 61–75; reprinted by permission.)

Figure 4.4. *(continued)*

By a combination of the above _____

By other means _____

6. Have you observed _____ using the system this month with
   peer _____ sister _____ brother _____ another person? _____ (Please
   name) _____
   If so, please describe: _____
   _____

7. Describe any particularly interesting communicative interaction that
   _____ has had with you or with someone else using the symbol
   system this month. _____
   _____

8. Are there specific problems or difficulties that _____ is experienc-
   ing with the system?
   Yes _____ No _____
   If yes, please indicate _____
   He cannot activate display panel successfully _____
   Confuses symbols _____ Which ones? _____
   Electronic/technical difficulties _____
   Were they repaired? Yes _____ No _____
   None _____
   Other _____

9. How frequently did you use the symbols/system with _____ this
   month?
   Daily, 5–7 days _____
   Sometimes, 1–4 days _____
   Not at all, 0 days _____

10. How have you used the system with _____ ?
    To ask a question _____
    To make a request _____
    To give instructions _____
    To clarify a verbalization made by _____ _____
    To label an item _____
    To answer a question _____
    To comment _____
    To respond to _____ 's communication _____

11. If you initiated a communication, how did _____ respond?
    Correctly acted upon your message _____
    Incorrectly acted upon your message _____
    Did not respond _____
    Other _____

Thank you.

served as teachers, discrete trial data (e.g., trials to criterion) on an individual's symbol learning did not provide a valid indication of augmented language development. We were interested in the participants' communicative use and knowledge of symbols. Specifically, we wanted to know both how the participants used the SAL during everyday interactions with adults and peers and what they had learned about the meanings of the symbols they used. Our assessment model, then, needed to include information about the participants' patterns of SAL use and the participants' symbol knowledge.

First, measures of SAL use needed to provide evidence of the participants' communicative patterns in different settings. Specifically, measures needed to provide information about with whom the individual communicated, how the individual communicated (i.e., modes), and what functions the individual's communications served, the success of the communications, as well as the effectiveness of the communication in sustaining the conversation. Second, although the patterns of communicative symbol use in functional contexts provided one dimension of detail about learning, these patterns did not ascertain what the individual knew about the meanings of the symbols they were using apart from the specific context. With the focus of instruction on communicative interaction, assessing what the individual learns about the symbols he uses permits the investigators to identify patterns of how he has abstracted symbol meaning from a new instructional context.

Measuring how everyday experience with the SAL influenced the language and communication skills of the participants therefore necessitated a multifaceted approach. We developed and implemented a model to capture an individual's communicative skills over time in these two areas (Romski & Sevcik, 1988b). Our model included two data collection components: 1) Communicative Use Probes (CUPs) and 2) Vocabulary Assessment Measures (VAMs).

Communicative Use Probes

Communicative Use Probes (CUPs), as we termed them, provided a window into the participants' use of the system in everyday interactions with adults and peers. CUPs were live observations, with accompanying audiotapes, of communicative interactions. Nonparticipant observers collected 37 CUPs in the home and school settings across the 2 years of the study. The nonparticipant observers were graduate research assistants who were taught to use the coding scheme by the investigators. We observed each participant 18 times for approximately 30 minutes per CUP during the study's first year. With the expansion to use in both home and school settings during the second year, we observed each participant in each of the two settings. These observations resulted in 19 CUPs, 9 in the original setting and 10 in the new setting. After consultation with parents and teachers, we chose not to collect CUP or VAM data at home during the summer, because of vacations and scheduling difficulties. Also, we did not have a comparable opportunity to collect data in a school setting on all the school-group participants during the summer.

We created the Communication Coding Scheme (CCS) (Romski & Sevcik, 1988b) to code each communicative event within the interactions we observed and recorded. The CCS was a four-digit cross-classified event coding scheme, which is shown in Table 4.5.

Each coded event included five types of information: the *partner* who interacted with the participant (adult, peer), the *role* of the participant in the communication (initiation, response), by what *mode* the participant was communicating (e.g., symbol, gesture, vocalization, physical manipulation), what *function* the participant's communication served (e.g., greeting, naming, answering), and the *success* (successful, unsuccessful) of the communication. Code definitions are listed in Table 4.6.

When a CUP had been completed, the nonparticipant observer used the audiotapes to supplement the online observations so that a complete gloss could be made of natural speech as well as the synthetic speech produced when lexigrams were activated. The observer then compiled a language transcript of the interaction using the Systematic Analysis of Language Transcripts (SALT) software program (Miller & Chapman, 1985). These transcripts incorporated the participants' and partners' communications and included the cross-classified event-based coding. On a post-hoc basis, using the compiled language transcripts as a database, participants' successful utterances were also coded on two additional dimensions: 1) *effectiveness*, in terms of the partner's subsequent communication, and 2) *vocabulary focus*.

In order to code effectiveness, three trained observers classified each utterance identified as successful from the transcript as *effective* or *not clearly effective*. Effective utterances were those in which the partner's response praised, repeated, commented on, expanded, or answered the participant's communication. Utterances classified as not clearly effective were those that met with a negative response by the partners (e.g., rejecting the response mode or the

Table 4.5. Communication Coding Scheme (CCS)

Code 1:	**Speaker Role, Partner**
1.000	Initiation, adult
2.000	Initiation, peer
3.000	Response, adult
4.000	Response, peer
Code 2:	**Mode**
0.W00	spoken word, intelligible
0.L00	symbol (SAL code)
0.G00	gesture
0.V00	vocalization
0.P00	physical manipulation
0.A00	symbol + gesture (SAL code)
0.B00	word + gesture
0.C00	vocalization + gesture
0.D00	symbol + vocalization (SAL code)
0.E00	symbol + vocalization + gesture (SAL code)
0.F00	physical manipulation + vocalization
0.H00	physical manipulation + word
Code 3:	**Communicative Function**
0.000	imitating
0.010	greeting
0.020	naming
0.030	requesting
0.040	attention directing
0.050	questioning
0.060	answering
0.070	affirming
0.080	negating
Code 4:	**Success**
0.00S	Successful
0.00U	Unsuccessful

From Romski, M.A., & Sevcik, R.A. (1988b). Augmentative communication system acquisition and use: A model for teaching and assessing progress. *NSSLHA Journal, 15,* 61–75; reprinted by permission.

communication message), were uninterpretable, or resulted in a response unrelated to the original event. (See Romski, Sevcik, Robinson, & Bakeman, 1994, for a detailed presentation.)

To code vocabulary conversational focus from the transcripts, participant utterances were initially classified as *referential, social-regulative, referential and social-regulative,* and *fully unclear.* An utterance had a referential focus if any of the speaker's acts focused

Table 4.6.   Communication Coding Scheme (CCS) definitions

Partner referred to the individuals with whom the participant communicates. *Adult* is a parent, teacher, or other such person (e.g, observer, grandparent), while *peer* is a youth in the school or a sibling.

Speaker role identified the character of the participant's communicative event in turn taking. An event was coded as an *Initiation* when it occurred at least 5 seconds after the last partner event. An event was coded as a *Response* when it was a reply to a partner communication occurring within 5 seconds of a partner turn. This distinction is based simply on the presence or absence of a prior communicative event by a partner because the research questions were directed to the flow of communication not the semantics of a specific topic.

The *Mode* of the event was coded to describe SAL and Non-SAL use. SAL codes encompassed all symbol uses including those that contained mode combinations (e.g., symbol + vocalization). Non-SAL codes collapse across four specific mode categories (i.e., gesture, physical manipulation, vocalization, spoken word) that were coded live during the CUPs (Romski & Sevcik, 1988b). The definitions of SAL and Non-SAL codes follow:

A *gesture* is defined as a point, reach, or other such movement made with the hands; a head nod; or a head shake to indicate something to another (adult/peer).

Physical manipulation is defined as an act of physically leading or guiding the adult/peer in some way to gain an outcome.

A *symbol* is defined as a visual-graphic representation.

A *vocalization* is defined as a sound or sequence of sounds that is not intelligible to the listener (coder) as a spoken word.

A *spoken word* is defined as a sound sequence that is understood by the listener (coder) to be a word.

Communication function referred to how the participant used the mode pragmatically.

Affirming is defined as agreeing with an utterance or confirming an utterance or behavior of the adult or peer partner.

Answering is defined as responding to a question or a comment from an adult or peer.

Attention directing is defined as engaging the attention of an adult or peer toward oneself or another person, object, or event.

Greeting is defined as using a salutation at meeting or at departing.

Imitating is defined as repeating exactly or partially what an adult or peer has said or done via speech or gesture.

Naming is defined as identifying an object or person spontaneously or in response to a "What's this" or "What are these" question.

Negating is defined as objecting to the behavior or verbalization/vocalization of an adult or peer; as declining an object, action, or event; or as denying the existence of something.

Questioning is defined as asking for information or a comment from an adult or peer.

Requesting is defined as asking for an item, action, or location, or asking someone to do something.

(continued)

Table 4.6. *(continued)*

Success referred to the ability of the participant to engage the partner in communication.

An utterance was *successful* if the partner to whom it was directed responded to the subject's utterance within 5 seconds.

Unsuccessful utterances occurred when the adult/peer to whom it was directed did not receive the message, failed to respond to the message, or did not interpret the message as a communication.

From Romski, M.A., & Sevcik, R.A. (1988b). Augmentative communication system acquisition and use: A model for teaching and assessing progress. *NSSLHA Journal, 15,* 61–75; reprinted by permission.

attention on an object or event by, for example, providing a name for or pointing toward a specific food. An utterance had a social-regulative focus if the speaker acted in a way to call attention to himself, his partner, or the communicative link between them. An utterance had both a referential and social-regulative focus if the speaker's communication met the criterion for each focus. An utterance was fully unclear if the observer was unable to ascribe specific content to at least one element of the utterance. (See Adamson, Romski, Deffebach, & Sevcik, 1992, for details.)

In total, 473 language transcripts (37 per participant, with the exception of GJ, who completed only 2 probes at home during Year 2 of the study for a total of 29) served as the 2-year database. From this database, 32,932 communicative utterances (mean per participant = 2,533) were coded and analyzed, and these data are discussed in Chapters 5 and 6.

Vocabulary Assessment Measures

Vocabulary Assessment Measures (VAMs) were a series of 10 structured tasks designed to determine what the participants had learned about the meanings of the symbols that they were using apart from the supporting contextual framework in which the symbols were used. Each task was administered by an investigator at school in a structured one-to-one assessment format outside of the communicative use setting of home or school. VAMs were first administered to gain a baseline measure of the participant's performance prior to the onset of the study and then at five regular intervals during each year of the study. These 10 tasks, listed in Table 4.7, included 4 measures of comprehension and 6 measures of production, as well as an opportunity to assess incidental learning of two skills that have been reported to emerge during augmented language experiences: 1) recognition of printed English

Table 4.7. Vocabulary assessment measures (VAMs)

Task	Stimuli	Response
Comprehension		
1.	Spoken word	Select photograph[a]
2.	Synthetic speech	Select photograph
3.	Symbol	Select photograph
4.	Printed word	Select photograph
Production		
1.	Photograph	Produce spoken word
2.	Symbol	Produce spoken word
3.	Photograph	Select symbol
4.	Spoken word	Select symbol
5.	Synthetic speech	Select symbol
6.	Printed word	Select symbol

From Romski, M.A., & Sevcik, R.A. (1988b). Augmentative communication system acquisition and use: A model for teaching and assessing progress. *NSSLHA Journal, 15,* 61–75; reprinted by permission.

[a]Selection is made from a choice of three foils and one target that remain consistent across all tasks.

words, and 2) intelligible production of spoken words. The procedures used to administer the 10 tasks are described in Table 4.8.

As can be seen in Table 4.8, we varied the stimuli presented in the tasks. When youth learn through visual *and* auditory modalities, the tasks used to measure comprehension and production are somewhat different than if learning takes place primarily through the auditory modality. Typically, cross-modal tasks (auditory to visual, visual to auditory) are used to assess spoken language abilities. For example, in a language comprehension task such as the PPVT–R (Dunn & Dunn, 1981), the auditory stimulus of a spoken word is given, and the participant is asked to respond by pointing to one of four line drawings. In contrast, in order to assess comprehension of visual symbols, the participant is shown a symbol and asked to identify its photographic match. This is an intramodal task (visual to visual). In a speech production task, the participant is shown a photograph and is asked to respond by saying the word (visual to auditory). In a symbol production task, the participant is shown a photograph and is asked to point to a symbol (visual to visual). In general, the demands placed on the participant are different (cross-modal versus intramodal). In addition, the response itself is different. In a spoken response, the participant must recall and coordinate the oral motor movements

Table 4.8. VAM Procedures for administering the 10 VAM tasks (Table 4.7)

Comprehension

All four comprehension tasks use photographic arrays of four 3-inch by 5-inch photographs to represent the stimuli.

1. Spoken word → Select photograph

   Materials: Photographic array, data sheets

   Procedure: E (examiner) places each array in front of P (participant) and says, "Show me [target word name]." P points to a photograph in the array. E records P's response and says, "Thank you."

2. Synthetic speech → Select photograph

   Materials: Photographic array, communication device, data sheets

   Procedure: With the display panel facing E, E places the photographic array in front of P. E says, "Show me [presses target item]." E records P's response and says, "Thank you."

3. Symbol → Select photograph

   Materials: Photographic array, packet of participant's lexigrams (symbols), data sheets

   Procedure: E places the photographic array in front of P and presents the target lexigram. E says, "Show me [the target lexigram]," as she points to the lexigram. E does not say the spoken-word name for the lexigram. E records P's response and says, "Thank you."

4. Printed word → Select photograph

   Materials: Photographic array, packet of printed English words, data sheets

   Procedure: E places the photographic array in front of P and shows the printed English word. E says, "Show me [the target printed word]," as she points to the printed word. E does not say the spoken-word name for the printed word. E records P's response and says, "Thank you."

Production

1. Photograph → Produce spoken word

   Materials: Tape recorder, audiotape, photographic array, data sheets

   Procedure: E begins the audiotape recording by identifying P, date, and task. E then presents each photograph of the target item (following the sequence on the data sheet) and says, "What is this?" If the response is unintelligible or there is no response, E says, "[item name]. Say [item name]." (E does not transcribe P's response on the data sheet. Audiotaped responses are transcribed by an independent speech-language pathologist.)

2. Symbol → Produce spoken word

   Materials: Tape recorder, audiotape, packet of participant's lexigrams (symbols), data sheets

   Procedure: E begins the audiotape recording by identifying P, date, and task. E then presents each lexigram of the target item (following the sequence on the data sheet) and says, "What is this?" If the response is unintelligible or there is no response, E says, "[item name]. Say [item name]." (E does not transcribe P's response on the data sheet. Audiotaped responses are transcribed by an independent speech-language pathologist.)

3. Photograph → Select symbol

   Materials: Photographic array, packet of participant's lexigram (symbols), data sheets

(continued)

Table 4.8. *(continued)*

Procedures: E places a lexigram in front of P and shows P a photograph of the target item. E says, "Show me this [the target lexigram]," as she points to the photograph. E records P's response and says, "Thank you."

4. Spoken word → Select symbol

Materials: Packet of participant's lexigrams (symbols), data sheets

Procedures: E places a lexigram in front of P. E says, "Show me [target item name]." E records P's response and says, "Thank you."

5. Synthetic speech → Select symbol

Materials: Packet of participant's lexigrams (symbols), communication device, data sheets

Procedures: With the display panel facing E, E places the lexigram in front of P. E says, "Show me [presses target item]." E records P's response and says, "Thank you."

6. Printed word → Select symbol

Materials: Packet of participant's lexigrams (symbols), packet of printed English words, data sheets

Procedures: E places the lexigram in front of P and presents the target printed word. E says, "Show me this [the target item]" as she points to it. E records P's response and says, "Thank you."

---

necessary to produce a word. In a symbol response, the participant must coordinate the manual motor movement necessary to point to a selection. These differences must be acknowledged and included in assessments for augmented language learning.

Our assessment model provides a comprehensive approach for monitoring communicative symbol development and use at home and at school. This method offers an approach whereby change in both communicative use and symbol knowledge may be assessed. The procedures can be adapted easily for practical use in educational and clinical settings by incorporating CUPs and VAMs as a way of measuring a variety of dimensions of symbol knowledge.

REFERENCES

Adamlab. (1988). *Wolf manual.* Wayne, MI: Author.

Adamson, L.B., Romski, M.A., Deffebach, K., & Sevcik, R.A. (1992). Symbol vocabulary and the focus of conversations: Augmenting language development for youth with mental retardation. *Journal of Speech and Hearing Research, 35,* 1333–1344.

Beukelman, D.R., & Mirenda, P. (1992). *Augmentative and alternative communication: Management of severe communication disorders in children and adults.* Baltimore: Paul H. Brookes Publishing Co.

Brady, N., & McLean, L. (1996). Arbitrary symbol learning by adults with severe mental retardation: Comparison of lexigrams and printed words. *American Journal on Mental Retardation, 100,* 423–427.

Brady, N., & Saunders, K. (1991). Considerations in the effective teaching of object-to-symbol matching. *Augmentative and Alternative Communication, 7,* 112–116.

Calculator, S. (1988). Promoting the acquisition and generalization of communication skills by augmented speakers with mental retardation. *Augmentative and Alternative Communication, 4,* 94–103.

Dunn, L.M., & Dunn, L.M. (1981). *Peabody Picture Vocabulary Test—Revised.* Circle Pines, MN: American Guidance Service.

Fristoe, M., & Lloyd, L.L. (1979). Nonspeech communication. In N.R. Ellis (Ed.), *Handbook of mental deficiency: Psychological theory and research* (pp. 401–430). Hillsdale, NJ: Lawrence Erlbaum Associates.

Higginbotham, D.J., Drazek, A., & Sussman, J. (1995). *The effect of experience on the single-word intelligibility and discourse comprehension of synthetic speech.* Unpublished manuscript.

Johnson, D. (1981). *The Picture Communication Symbols, book I.* Solana Beach, CA: Mayer-Johnson Co.

Johnson, D. (1985). *The Picture Communication Symbols, book II.* Solana Beach, CA: Mayer-Johnson Co.

Locke, P., & Mirenda, P. (1988). A computer-supported communication approach for a nonspeaking child with severe visual and cognitive impairments. *Augmentative and Alternative Communication, 4,* 15–22.

Miller, J., & Chapman, R. (1985). *Systematic Analysis of Language Transcripts (SALT).* [Computer program]. Madison: University of Wisconsin.

Mirenda, P., & Beukelman, D. (1987). A comparison of speech synthesis intelligibility with listeners from three age groups. *Augmentative and Alternative Communication, 4,* 120–128.

Mirenda, P., & Beukelman, D. (1990). A comparison of intelligibility among natural speech and seven speech synthesizers with listeners from three age groups. *Augmentative and Alternative Communication, 6,* 61–68.

Oliver, C., & Halle, J. (1982). Language training in the everyday environment: Teaching functional signs to a retarded child. *Journal of The Association for the Severely Handicapped, 7,* 50–62.

Reichle, J., York, J., & Sigafoos, J. (1991). *Implementing augmentative and alternative communication: Strategies for learners with severe disabilities.* Baltimore: Paul H. Brookes Publishing Co.

Romski, M.A., & Sevcik, R.A. (1988a). Augmentative and alternative communication: Considerations for individuals with severe intellectual disabilities. *Augmentative and Alternative Communication, 4,* 83–93.

Romski, M.A., & Sevcik, R.A. (1988b). Augmentative communication system acquisition and use: A model for teaching and assessing progress. *NSSLHA Journal, 15,* 61–75.

Romski, M.A., Sevcik, R.A., & Pate, J.L. (1988). The establishment of symbolic communication in persons with severe retardation. *Journal of Speech and Hearing Disorders, 53,* 94–107.

Romski, M.A., Sevcik, R.A., Robinson, B., & Bakeman, R. (1994). Adult-directed communications of youth with mental retardation using the

System for Augmenting Language. *Journal of Speech and Hearing Research, 38*, 902–912.

Romski, M.A., Sevcik, R.A., & Rumbaugh, D.M. (1985). Retention of symbolic communication skills by severely mentally retarded persons. *American Journal of Mental Deficiency, 89*, 313–316.

Romski, M.A., White, R.A., Millen, C.A., & Rumbaugh, D.M. (1984). Effects of computer-keyboard teaching on the symbolic communication of severely retarded persons: Five case studies. *Psychological Record, 34*, 39–54.

Rumbaugh, D.M. (Ed.). (1977). *Language learning by a chimpanzee: The LANA Project*. New York: Academic Press.

Savage-Rumbaugh, E.S., McDonald, K., Sevcik, R.A., Hopkins, W., & Rubert, E. (1986). Spontaneous symbol acquisition and communicative use by pygmy chimpanzees *(Pan paniscus). Journal of Experimental Psychology: General, 115*, 211–235.

Savage-Rumbaugh, E.S., Rumbaugh, D.M., & Boysen, S. (1980). Do apes have language? *American Scientist, 40*, 40–51.

Savage-Rumbaugh, E.S., Sevcik, R.A., Brakke, K., Rumbaugh, D.M., & Greenfield, P. (1990). Symbols: Their communicative use, comprehension, and combination by bonobos *(Pan paniscus)*. In L.P. Lipsitt & C. Rovee-Collier (Eds.), *Advances in infancy research* (Vol. 6, pp. 221–278). Norwood, NJ: Ablex.

Sevcik, R.A, Romski, M.A., Watkins, R., & Deffebach, K. (1995). Adult partner-augmented communication input to youth with mental retardation using the System for Augmenting Language (SAL). *Journal of Speech and Hearing Research, 38*, 902–912.

Sevcik, R.A., Romski, M.A., & Wilkinson, K. (1991). Roles of graphic symbols in the language acquisition process for persons with severe cognitive disabilities. *Augmentative and Alternative Communication, 7*, 161–170.

Snyder-McLean, L., Solomonson, B., McLean, J., & Sack, S. (1984). Structuring joint action routines: A strategy for facilitating communication and language development in the classroom. *Seminars in Speech and Language, 5*, 213–228.

Unicorn Engineering. (1985). *Expanded Keyboard Model 1*. Oakland, CA: Author.

Warren, S., & Rogers-Warren, A. (1985). *Teaching functional language*. Baltimore: University Park Press.

Words+, Inc. (1985). *Words+ Portable Voice II user's manual*. Sunnyvale, CA: Author.

Yoder, P., Kaiser, A., & Alpert, K. (1991). An exploratory study of the interaction between language teaching methods and child characteristics. *Journal of Speech and Hearing Research, 34*, 155–167.

Yoder, D., & Miller, J. (1972). What we may know and what we can do: Input toward a system. In J. McLean, D. Yoder, & R. Schiefelbusch (Eds.), *Language intervention with the retarded: Developing strategies* (pp. 89–110). Baltimore: University Park Press.

PART II

Research to Practice

Chapter 5

Language and Communication Achievements

Communicative Use of the System for Augmenting Language

Youth with significant mental retardation often evidence difficulties conveying information to, and interacting with, adults and other youth in a variety of contexts (Knopp & Recchia, 1990). From a societal perspective, perhaps the most important accomplishment the participants in our study could attain would be the facile use of the SAL for communication across a range of partners in a variety of natural settings. Communication achievements of this nature can lead the way for these youth to function more independently in educational, family, community, and, eventually, employment activities.

A concrete example of how use of the SAL permitted one participant to convey information to his mother is illustrated in the following observation gleaned from the QUEST, the questionnaire regularly completed by parents and teachers. At the end of the investigation's first school year, TE's mother reported that she had not planned to send him to the county's summer school program that year. The week before summer school was to begin, however, TE used his speech-output communication device repeatedly over a period of several days to say, "SCHOOL." When his mother asked him, "Who do you want to see at school?," she reported that he responded with the vocal approximation of what his mother interpreted to be his teacher's name. After a week or so of TE continuing this type of exchange, TE's mother called his teacher, explained what TE had communicated to her with his SAL, and asked if he could attend summer school. TE attended the school program that summer because he was able to convey his desire to do so through the use of his communication system, the SAL.

What skills contribute to making a participant's communications functional in such social interactions? Every communicative event must accomplish two goals in order for communications to be functional, that is, to continue the flow of the conversation. As discussed in the previous chapter, first, the participant's attempt at communication must be clear enough to open the communicative channel with a potential partner; that is, it must be successful in engaging the partner in communication. Second, the communicative partner must be able to interpret the content of the message and respond to it in order to continue the flow of communication; that is, it must be effective. A number of intrinsic and extrinsic factors are likely to affect the success and effectiveness of communications when using the SAL. These factors include the communicative partners, the modes of communication, the instructional environments, and the extant skills of the participants themselves.

Given the types of experiences the participants in our study encountered, what was the range of communication skills they actually achieved across the 2 years? First and foremost, the immersion and use of the SAL in the participants' natural communicative environments offered a viable opportunity for the language and communication development of each individual participant. Individual participant achievements ranged from the communicative use with adults of a modest set of 20–35 symbols to the use of well over 100 symbols in complex ways for communication with familiar and unfamiliar adult and peer partners.

Chapter 5 is devoted to a characterization of the ways in which the participants used the SAL to communicate with adults and peers, from the introduction of their first symbol through the end of the study. In Chapter 6, we then detail the youth's vocabulary mastery and resulting gains, including improvements in speech production and printed English word recognition. Both chapters include directions for practice that resulted from our findings.

INITIATING SYMBOL USE

As discussed in Chapter 4, the participants initially encountered a single symbol on their communication devices, chosen by their parents or teacher in collaboration with us, the investigators. The communicative partners focused on choosing a symbol that would be highly motivating to the individual as well as readily incorporated into the initial communication setting of a mealtime situation. Using the same standard, a second highly motivating symbol was chosen. Table 5.1 lists the first two symbols each participant had on his display panel.

All 13 participants immediately and successfully activated their individual symbol on the speech-output device during the mealtime setting in which it was introduced. An example of a participant's first SAL use is provided in Table 5.2. As can be seen, use was appropriate and was structured by the partner during the activity. Both parents and teachers reported that the participants seemed to be intrigued by the speech-output communication device and its voice. JL's mother, for example, reported that he would sit in his room for extended periods of time, touch a symbol, listen to the synthetic word it produced, and then touch it again.

It is possible, although unlikely, that the participants had just learned a conditioned response: Touch the symbol; receive an item. Thus, the more important symbol introduction came with the presentation of the second symbol, because this required the participant to distinguish Symbol 1 from Symbol 2 and to appropriately pair each symbol with its referent. When the second symbol

Table 5.1. First and second symbols selected for each participant

Participant	First symbol	Second symbol
Home instruction group		
DE	Ice cream	Cheese
BB	Coca Cola	Hot dog
TF	Ice cream	Ketchup
JL	Raisin	Peanut butter
KH	Peanut butter	Kool Aid
DC	Milk	Ketchup
School instruction group		
TE	Ice cream	Milk
FG	Chocolate milk	Toast
KW	Kool Aid	Toast
EC	Bread	Peanut butter
MH	Potato chip	Bread
JA	Potato chip	Bread
GJ	Ice cream	Juice

Table 5.2. Example of a participant's first use of the SAL

T	What do you want?
S	XX {ICE CREAM}.
T	Go get it.
T	Get your {ICE CREAM}.
T	What is Jimmy eating?
S	{ICE CREAM}.

Transcript is in SALT format, although SALT conventions have been removed for ease of understanding. T = teacher, S = student, XX = unintelligible vocalization, { } = lexigram use.

was introduced, none of the participants encountered difficulty in distinguishing the symbols from each other. They all employed the first and second symbols correctly during mealtime, as shown in the example in Table 5.3.

Beginning with a Single Symbol

Participants began the study with a single symbol because of findings from our previous study about initial symbol learning. The participants in this study immediately understood what to do and used the first symbol and then the second symbol appropriately. They performed differently enough for us to question the validity of our earlier hypothesis.

Perhaps it is not essential to begin augmented language learning with a single symbol when a naturalistic instructional approach, such as the SAL, is employed. Research at the Language Research Center (LRC) with an infant bonobo (*Pan paniscus*) demonstrated that the infant was able to choose appropriate individual symbols for communication in a natural setting from an array of well over 100 symbol possibilities. Despite this formidable task, she did not evidence positional biases and could select a symbol of interest from different displays (Sevcik, Savage-Rumbaugh, & Rumbaugh, 1996).

Table 5.3. Example of the use of Symbols 1 and 2 during the same interaction

T	What are you drinking?
S	{MILK}.
T	Right.
S	{ICE CREAM}.
=	T got up to go and S noticed, commenting or directing her to get ice cream.
S	{ICE CREAM}.
T	I knew what you were going to say.

Transcript is in SALT format, although SALT conventions have been removed for ease of understanding. T = teacher, S = student, { } = lexigram use, = = comment.

Overall, the issue of building a vocabulary, particularly for individuals with significant mental retardation, is complex. At the very least, it requires a consideration of what symbols should make up the lexicon, how many symbols should be introduced at one time, and where they should be positioned on the display. Given our own research experience, our approach to building vocabulary was deliberately cautious. Our participants' performance helped set the stage for the expansion of their lexicons.

Building a Vocabulary for Use

When all participants had used the two symbols successfully for 3–4 weeks, we simultaneously introduced 10 more symbols, for a total of 12, that represented additional foods, drinks, and utensils appropriate for the mealtime situation. The addition of these symbols permitted our participants to communicate about a broader range of items in the mealtime setting. With the introduction of these 10 symbols, we began to observe some subtle differences in how rapidly and appropriately each participant used these new symbols. Some participants readily incorporated the appropriate use of all 10 new symbols into their repertoire within a few weeks. A few participants (BB, FG, GJ, and KH), however, encountered some difficulty with the larger set of symbols. In retrospect, perhaps continuing the one-new-symbol-at-a-time approach may have been appropriate for this subset of youth. In Chapter 6, we discuss more fully how we assessed these performance differences and the distinct achievement patterns that emerged in the participants.

Expanding the Lexicon

At this point, the participants' 12-symbol vocabularies consisted exclusively of referential symbols. We wanted to expand the lexicon available to them to include symbols that represented another referential category: leisure items such as TV and MAGAZINE. When a participant comprehended 8 of the 12 symbols on his display (measured via the comprehension tasks on the VAM), we added six individually chosen leisure items to his vocabulary. The point at which this addition took place varied, depending on the participant's skills (range = after VAM 3 – after VAM 10; mean = after VAM 5). Nine of the participants had leisure vocabulary items on their displays by the end of the study's first year.

In addition, parents and teachers urged us to add a new category of symbols to represent social-regulative meanings, such as PLEASE, HELP, and THANK YOU. They felt that the addition of these symbols would permit a broader and more appropriate use of their

children's and students' symbol vocabulary. Some parents remarked, for example, that they wished their children to express
themselves by using the same terms indicating politeness that they
expected from their other children. We were hesitant to do this
because traditional clinical practice suggested that referential symbols were concrete and thus more easily learned by individuals
with significant mental retardation than were symbols repre-
senting abstract concepts. We were concerned, however, that if we
did not listen to their advice, we would jeopardize their interest and
continued participation. Because the participants' instructional experience (and our research project) truly lay in the hands of these
adults who served as communicative models, we responded positively to their request. Because we were still concerned about the
youth's ability to incorporate such symbols, we differentiated the
social-regulative symbols from the referential symbols by placing
them on one side of the display panel.

Social-Regulative Symbol Use

Along with our colleagues Adamson and Deffebach (Adamson,
Romski, Deffebach, & Sevcik, 1992), we examined how the introduction of these social-regulative symbols influenced the participants' conversations. The outcomes certainly surprised us: We
found that these social-regulative symbols were used as soon as
they were available on an individual's display panel. Immediately,
their availability expanded the participants' conversations both at
home and at school. Although the quality of SAL communications
was altered, the introduction of social-regulative symbols did not
increase the overall amount of SAL use. Given that all participants
were provided with social-regulative symbols following referential
symbols, we do not know the effect of the order of their introduction; that is, we may have observed a different pattern of acquisition
and use if the symbol types had been presented in a different order
or simultaneously.

Perhaps, even more important, when social-regulative symbols became available, they were combined with other symbols to
form semantically more complex utterances (e.g., "MORE MILK
PLEASE") (Wilkinson, Romski, & Sevcik, 1994). Overall, then, because the participants' lexicons now included social-regulative
terms, their ability to regulate interpersonal exchanges using culturally appropriate ways of communicating was greatly enhanced.

The lexicon made available to our participants appeared to
shape the social nature of their interactions as well as the content
of their communications. The use of a broad range of symbols may

have influenced the participants' ability to engage in communication with multiple partners in varied social contexts and also influenced the partners' perceptions of the participants' social competence. The adults were perhaps sensitized to vocabulary issues because they also used the system as they served as the participants' communicative models. Needless to say, our parents' and teachers' contributions to this finding about the lexicon should not be underestimated. In a broad sense, this speaks to the importance of input from participants in investigations such as this.

COMMUNICATIVE USE OF THE SAL

As we were developing the participants' lexicon and its potential for use, we were simultaneously observing how they used the SAL on a regular basis to communicate. As discussed in Chapter 4, the event-based observational coding scheme, the Communication Coding Scheme (CCS) (Romski & Sevcik, 1988), captured the many dimensions of SAL use in the participants' everyday environments. It permitted us to characterize each utterance during an observation with respect to partner, role, mode, function, success, and effectiveness. From each observation, we created language transcripts using the Systematic Analysis of Language Transcripts (SALT) program (Miller & Chapman, 1985) to characterize each utterance. The transcripts of these interactions provided a window by which we could characterize the ways in which the participants employed their SALs.

The overwhelming majority of the participants' communications, 96%, were directed to adults, and only 4% were directed to peers. This finding is not surprising, however, because the instructional environments placed a heavy focus on interactions with adult partners. Given the distinct differences in quantity alone, we examine the participants' communications to these two types of partners separately.

Communicating with Adults

Along with our colleagues Robinson and Bakeman (Romski, Sevcik, Robinson, & Bakeman, 1994), we described the adult-directed communications of our participants, which are illustrated in the photograph in Figure 5.1. First, we characterized the mode (SAL and Non-SAL) of the communication. Then we assessed how successfully and effectively the participants employed the SAL with their adult partners. We also considered factors related to success and

Figure 5.1. FG communicates with his older sister during a family dinner. (Photograph by Rose A. Sevcik.)

effectiveness of SAL use, including communicative role in the dialogue and pragmatic function served by the communication.

SAL and Non-SAL Communications   Our school-age participants already had well-established ways to communicate with others (Romski, Sevcik, Reumann, & Pate, 1989). As detailed in Chapter 3, prior to the introduction of the SAL, participants generally used vocalizations and pointing gestures to direct their partners' attention to themselves. Their partners (here parents and teachers) then inferred their wants and needs. Although partners usually responded to these vocal and gestural communications of the participants, the communications often were not effective; that is, the partners typically negated the communications. For example, after TE vocalized unintelligibly, his teacher responded by saying, "I don't understand you."

After the SAL was introduced, we examined our participants' use of SAL communications and their use of Non-SAL communications (i.e., vocalizations, gestures, physical manipulations, or their combinations as defined in Table 4.5). It is not surprising that, rather than adopting the SAL as their only form of communication, our participants incorporated its use in their existing communicative repertoires and used the SAL in an average of 37% of their communications. Their use of natural, unintelligible vocalizations *did not* decrease after the introduction of the communication device, and these accounted for over 80% of their Non-SAL communications. As shown in Figure 5.2, these Non-SAL modes were used primarily to gain the attention of their partners (37%) and to answer questions directed to the participant (27%). In contrast, SAL use functioned to request (45%), to name (37%), and to answer questions (11.7%).

SAL and Non-SAL Communicative Success Our observations revealed that the overwhelming majority of our participants' communications (88%), both SAL and Non-SAL, were successful; that is, they obtained a response from the partner. Thus, the participants were able to get a response, regardless of their mode of communication. This finding points out a striking difference between our

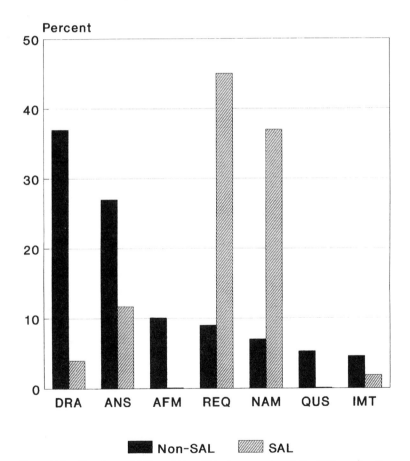

Figure 5.2. Functions of SAL and Non-SAL utterances to adults. (DRA = directing attention, ANS = answering, AFM = affirming, REQ = requesting, NAM = naming, QUS = questioning, IMT = imitating.)

participants and the individuals whom we had previously studied who lived in a residential setting. In the residence, communicative success was not a given. TS, for example, was sitting on a couch in the living room. Next to her on the couch was another resident's shoe. A caregiver was looking for this shoe. TS repeatedly vocalized and pointed next to her. After about 10 minutes of searching, the caregiver found the shoe sitting where TS had been pointing and vocalizing. The caregiver asked, "TS, why didn't you tell me the shoe was right here next to you?" TS just smiled. Even though the opportunity to engage in communication was present, the (potential) communicative partner did not acknowledge or respond to TS's communicative attempt. It should be noted, however, that the participants' partners in the SAL study had been sensitized to the importance of varied modes of communication.

When responding to their partners' communications, participants were successful 92% of the time at home and school, regardless of whether they used the SAL. In general, responses were less variable across home and school environments than were initiations. When they initiated communications with the SAL, participants were slightly more successful in communicating at school than at home (85% versus 66%). Non-SAL initiations functioned in the reverse: Participants were more successful with Non-SAL initiations at home (82%) than at school (73%).

SAL and Non-SAL Communicative Effectiveness A communication was effective when the partner responded to a successful communication in a way that continued the conversation. Specifically, successful utterances were judged effective when a partner's response acknowledged, praised, repeated, commented on, expanded, and/or answered the participant's communication. It is important to note that our participants' communications were always more effective when they used the SAL than when they did not use it. In addition, participants were more effective when they initiated communications than when they responded to communications initiated by others. Unlike success of communication, the two instructional environments, home and school, did not seem to affect communicative effectiveness.

What made SAL communications more effective than Non-SAL communications? In all likelihood, it was the clarity provided by the use of a conventional form of communication. The participants' SAL use permitted the partners to understand the information the participant was trying to convey to the partner and respond to it, thus continuing the conversational exchange.

SAL Use Over Time: Maintenance and Generalization Two important, and related, dimensions of the participants' adult-directed communications relate to SAL use over time. These two additional dimensions—maintenance and generalization—were a focus of the study in the second year.

For our purposes, we operationally defined *maintenance* as continuing to use the SAL to communicate with adults in the instructional environment in which it was introduced. When participants had used the SAL for 1 school year in their initial instructional environment, we assessed how well they maintained SAL use with adults in this setting after the summer break. When school began again in the fall, we immediately assessed their maintenance in the initial environment. We found a positive relationship in each participant's successful use of the SAL between Year 1 and Year 2 of the study. This finding indicates that participants who were successful communicators with the SAL during the first year continued their success in the second year. Communicative partners in home and school instructional settings promoted the participants' maintenance of successful and effective SAL use during the second school year as well as they had in the first year.

In addition to continuing SAL use in the first environment, we initiated SAL use in a second environment. We operationally defined *generalization* as the transfer of communicative use of the SAL to a second instructional environment, either home or school, depending on the initial instructional environment. Regardless of the initial environment, participants generalized their successful and effective SAL use from the instructional environment to the second environment.

Overall, then, it appeared that home and school were equally good introductory environments. The differences between them in communicative use, maintenance, and generalization were minimal. There is, however, an important caution about this finding related to parental perception. When home was the initial setting, and when the use of the system was extended to include school in Year 2, some parents reported that, as the second year progressed, they wanted to turn the responsibility for using the SAL over to the participants' teachers. When we queried them about their feelings, they said that they thought the teachers were better prepared, as formal educators, to teach their children how to communicate than they were. The other group of parents, those whose children had used the SAL at school during the first year of the investigation, eagerly welcomed the SAL's introduction into their homes and did not report the same feelings. Given the parents' comments, then, school may be a more facilitative environment in which to begin SAL use, followed by use in the home once the individual is successfully communicating with the SAL.

Communicating with Peers

As mentioned earlier in this chapter, only 4% of the participants' communications were directed to peers. Along with our colleague Wilkinson (Romski, Sevcik, & Wilkinson, 1994), we examined the peer-directed communications of our participants. Figure 5.3 is a photograph of a peer-directed communication. Although all participants had opportunities for peer interaction in school, home opportunities were more variable across participants. At home, all but one of the participants (KW) had an opportunity to interact with siblings. In general, there were more limited opportunities

Figure 5.3. TE and a peer without disabilities communicate in the classroom. (Photograph by Rose A. Sevcik.)

for participants to interact with peers, with and without disabilities, than with adults. Opportunities were limited for two reasons.
First, often peers with disabilities also had significant communication difficulties. Second, at the time of this study, interactions
with peers without disabilities were frequently confined to specific activities.

A review of all peer-directed utterances across participants
indicated that one participant (KH) produced no peer-directed
communications. A very small number (1%) of peer-directed communications were produced by three participants (BB, FG, GJ),
although their opportunities for peer interaction appeared comparable to those of other participants. Overall, peer-directed communications constituted less than 1% (0.3%) of all communications that
these three participants produced during our observations. These
15 communications are listed and characterized in Table 5.4. Of the
communications, 10 were Non-SAL initiations that functioned to
direct the attention of the peer partner, and one Non-SAL utterance
was a response that directed the attention of the peer partner. All
11 Non-SAL utterances were unintelligible vocalizations, and half
of these were successful. The remaining four utterances (produced
by FG) were three successful SAL answers to a question and one

Table 5.4. Peer-directed communications of BB, FG, and GJ

Partici-pant	Instruc-tional setting, year	Commu-nicative role	Communicative function	Communicative mode	Commu-nicative success	Commu-nicative effectiveness
BB	H, YR1	I	Attention directing	Non-SAL	U	-
	H, YR1	I	Attention directing	Non-SAL	U	-
	S, YR2	I	Attention directing	Non-SAL	U	-
	S, YR2	I	Attention directing	Non-SAL	U	-
	S, YR2	I	Attention directing	Non-SAL	SU	E
FG	S, YR1	I	Attention directing	Non-SAL	SU	E
	S, YR1	R	Attention directing	Non-SAL	SU	E
	S, YR1	R	Attention directing	SAL	SU	E
	S, YR1	R	Answering	SAL	SU	NCE
	S, YR1	R	Answering	SAL	SU	E
	S, YR1	R	Answering	SAL	SU	E
GJ	S, YR1	I	Attention directing	Non-SAL	U	-
	S, YR1	I	Attention directing	Non-SAL	U	-
	H, YR2	I	Attention directing	Non-SAL	SU	E
	H, YR2	I	Attention directing	Non-SAL	SU	E

H = home, S = school, I = initiation, R = response, U = unsuccessful, SU = successful, E = effective, NCE = not clearly effective, - = not coded.

successful SAL attention-directing utterance. Three of these successful communications were also judged to be effective.

The peer-directed communications produced by the nine other participants (JL, DE, TE, JA, MH, DC, EC, TF, and KW) were also a very small number of their total observed communications (6%). Table 5.5 provides examples of peer-directed communications.

SAL and Non-SAL Communications Communications were directed to peers with and without disabilities alike, although the majority (81%) were directed to peers without disabilities. Participants used Non-SAL modes to communicate with peers more often than the SAL. The Non-SAL modes they employed for peer-directed communications were consistent with the Non-SAL modes they used for adult-directed communications (see previous discussion). These modes included vocalizations (81%), followed by single words (11%), gestures (7%), and physical manipulation (1%). In general, the participants were more likely to respond to communications by their peers than to initiate communications with them. It is interesting that SAL and Non-SAL modes were used for slightly different communicative functions. Although SAL and Non-SAL modes were used primarily to answer an-

Table 5.5. Two examples of peer-directed communications

Example 1. Participant at lunch in the school cafeteria with peer without a disability
D Hi there.
D What are you eating?
P XX.
D Pizza.
D Is it good?
P {GOOD}.
D What do you need to eat with?
P {FORK}.
D Good, fork.
D Ok, let's eat.

Example 2. Participant at home after school having a snack with brother
B What are you going to eat?
P {ICE CREAM}
B {ICE CREAM} sounds good.
P XX.
= P vocally approximates "I want to do."
B Wait no you can't do this.
P XX.
B No!

P = participant, D = typical peer, B = brother without a disability, XX = unintelligible vocalization, { } = lexigram, = = comment.

other's communication (given the high percentage of responses), SAL utterances were largely informational, fulfilling the communicative functions of answering (58%), naming (14%), and requesting + questioning (14%), followed by greeting + attention directing (11%), and imitating (3%). In contrast, Non-SAL modes were used to answer (45%), greet + direct attention (35%), followed by requesting + questioning (9%), imitating (9%), and naming (2%). Functions of SAL and Non-SAL communications are illustrated in Figure 5.4.

SAL and Non-SAL Communicative Success Of our participants' peer-directed utterances, 75% were successful. SAL use increased the percentage of successful peer-directed utterances, particularly

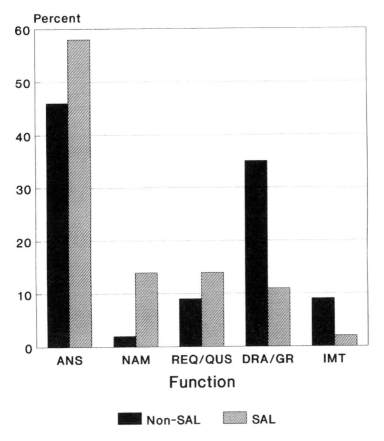

Figure 5.4. Functions of SAL and Non-SAL utterances used with peers. (ANS = answering, NAM = naming, REQ= requesting, QUS = questioning, DRA = directing attention, GR = greeting, IMT = imitating.)

when participants interacted with other students with disabilities. The SAL appeared to facilitate communication when both peers had a developmental disability and used the SAL for communication. Participants were more successful when they responded to a peer's communication than when they initiated one themselves. This finding, however, was twice as strong for interactions with peers without disabilities than for interactions with peers with disabilities. It may be that the abilities of peers without disabilities to continue topics and maintain conversations beyond two or three turns contributed to this finding.

SAL and Non-SAL Communicative Effectiveness The majority of the participants' successful communications to peers were effective; that is, the partner responded to the communication. Just as with the participants' adult-directed communications, SAL communications were more effective than Non-SAL communications. For example, JA saw an old friend who would not stop talking. JA used his SAL to say, "NO BE QUIET," in order to get his friend to pay attention to what he wanted to say.

Communications were also more likely to be effective when the partner was a typically developing peer than when the partner was another youth with a disability. Sometimes, perhaps because of their own communication disorders, peers with disabilities did not respond to communications from other peers with disabilities.

SAL and Non-SAL Communications to Peer Tutors Three of the participants (MH, TE, and TF) also interacted with peer tutors. These peer tutors received instruction prior to interacting with the participants that provided them with information about disabilities and with strategies for interacting with the participants using the SAL. We were interested in whether or not the participants' communications to their peer tutors were different from their communications to other peers without disabilities and to their siblings. The most striking difference was in the use of SAL: More than half of these three participants' communications to their peer tutors were SAL-based. In striking contrast, less than 10% of their communications to other peers without disabilities and to siblings were SAL-based. The peer tutors also encouraged and modeled SAL communications. For example, one day, a peer tutor was communicating with TF when a friend of the tutor joined them. The friend started talking to the peer tutor but ignored TF. The peer tutor said, "This is the way we talk," pointing to the SAL. His friend responded by saying he did not know how to use it. The peer tutor quickly said, "It's easy. You touch it and it talks for you. TF will show you." The conversation then continued, with all three using the SAL to talk. Although they initiated more communications with peers and siblings than with peer tutors, the majority of their communications were responses and functioned as answers to questions.

Character of Peer-Directed Communications Overall, the character of the participants' peer-directed communications were consistent with what we found regarding their adult-directed communications: SAL-based communications were an effective way of conveying successful messages of informational content. It does appear, however, that increasing the opportunities to interact with peers might require special attention. For example, we did not assess whether all peer partners were receptive to the communications of our participants. In fact, the peer-tutor findings, coupled with the research of others (Goldstein & Kaczmarek, 1991; Hunt, Alwell, & Goetz, 1991), suggest that interventions specifically directed toward facilitating peer communication may be necessary to increase such communications. Because inclusion in general education activities is now an educational focus, this is an aspect of intervention that definitely requires more attention.

PARTNER USE OF THE SAL

As highlighted in Chapter 4, one component of the participants' naturalistic instructional experience was that partners provided communication input using symbols. The literature, however, provides very little information about how augmented input should be presented for participants learning an augmented language system such as the SAL. By specifying how partners were to employ symbols and model SAL use in their communications with participants, we were able to analyze the augmented linguistic environment that the participants actually experienced.

Along with our colleagues Deffebach and Watkins (Sevcik, Romski, Watkins, & Deffebach, 1995), we used a portion of our SALT language-transcript database to examine the adult partners' use of the SAL during the interactions. In order to gain a description of the partners' communications, we calculated their mean length of utterance (MLU), the number of utterances of each partner during a speaking turn, and the number of partner utterances containing a symbol.

We also reliably coded each partner's symbol usage along two dimensions: directiveness and topic regulation. We defined *partner-directive communications* as including direct and indirect commands, overt corrections, forced-choice questions, repetitions of actual questions, and demand questions. With respect to topic regulation, we determined if the partner initiated a new topic, continued a topic, or changed a topic to follow the participant. Teaching strategies related to symbol use that the partners used were also detailed. To examine these, we calculated the number of lexigrams the partner used, the partner's repetition of lexigrams, and the position of the lexigram in the partner's utterance.

Mean partner MLU was 4.5. School partners dominated conversations more than home partners with a mean of 2.56 utterances per turn as compared with 1.81 for home partners. Partners integrated lexigram use in a small proportion of their verbal communications (mean = 9.3%). Significantly more lexigrams were used by partners communicating with BB, FG, GJ, and KH than by partners communicating with the other participants. As Chapter 3 indicated, these four participants exhibited poor oral-language comprehension skills; for these participants, the symbols clearly functioned as the primary input mode for both partners and participants. (See Chapter 7 for additional discussion.)

For all participants, both home and school partners tended to use symbols in the final position of their utterances (61%), such as in "Let's go OUTSIDE." Partners also recast a considerable proportion of their utterances (24%). School partners tended to use augmented input more directively than home partners (60% versus 26%). Although the quantity of partner symbol input was small, it was focused and salient in a manner that highlighted the use of symbols for our participants. It is important to note that both home and school adult partners, with relatively modest instruction in the use of the SAL, were quite skilled in presenting input in a salient and facilitative manner.

CONVEYING COMPLEX INFORMATION THROUGH THE SAL

Most studies of augmented language learning have focused on single-symbol learning only (Reichle, York, & Sigafoos, 1991; Romski & Sevcik, 1988). The few studies that have examined symbol combinations were instructional in nature and actually taught individuals to produce combinatorial usages (Carrier, 1974; Karlan et al., 1982). As the first year of SAL experience drew to a close, examination of the language transcript database revealed that meaningful and functional symbol combinations were spontaneously emerging in the repertoires of seven participants (DC, DE, JA, JL, KH, MH, and TE). For example, after one participant's mother asked him, "Do you want a piece of chicken?," he used lexigrams to reply, "WANT HOT DOG."

In collaboration with our colleague Wilkinson (Wilkinson, Romski, & Sevcik, 1994), we examined the symbol combinations that emerged spontaneously in the communications of our participants. From the language transcripts, we identified all of the participants' symbol combinations (total = 301, mean = 43 per participant, range = 8 – 122) and isolated them, along with contextual information, from the four utterances preceding and the four utterances following each combination. An example of symbol combination use is provided in Table 5.6. Based on the number of visual-symbol combinations each participant produced, we identified two naturally occurring groups: Combiners and Noncombiners. The seven participants (DC, DE, JA, JL, KH, MH, and TE) who produced more than five symbol combinations were classified as Combiners, and the six who produced fewer than five combinations (BB, EC, FG, GJ, KW, and TF) were classified as Noncombiners.

We used operational definitions of combinatorial symbol use from the LRC's nonhuman primate research (Greenfield & Savage-Rumbaugh, 1990) and information about semantic relations from the typical language development literature (Braine, 1976) to characterize the combinatorial symbol use that emerged in our participants. First, we described three aspects of their combinations: 1) the semantic relations expressed in the combinations, 2) the order of the symbols in the combinations, and 3) the participants' ability to generalize the use of the symbols in combinations. Next we examined the influence of the participants' assessed cognitive and linguistic knowledge base on their combinatorial usage. Finally, we explored the influence of their partners' symbol-combination input on the participants' symbol-combination usage.

Symbol Combinations

Of the participants' combinations, 89% conformed to Braine's (1976) relational category scheme, suggesting that their development of

Table 5.6. Example of symbol combination use reported by a communicative partner (teacher)

We had an interesting conversation one afternoon in the classroom as we were finishing some work. JA did not want to finish his work. He said, "NO," and, "BE QUIET." I told him he had to finish his work and he said, "GOODBYE." We continued working and in a few minutes he said, "I WANT OUTSIDE PLEASE." I told him he could go outside when he finished. JA completed the task and said, "FINISHED OUTSIDE PLEASE."

---

semantic relations resembled the very early word combinations of typically developing speaking children. Patterns of predominant semantic relations expressed in early spoken word combinations are shown in Table 5.7. Five participants employed consistent lexigram-ordering rules, indicating that at least some participants were capable of producing rule-governed combinations.

Relationship to Earlier Performance on Standardized Assessments of Speech Comprehension We were also interested in whether standardized assessments of the comprehension of spoken word combinations, administered at the onset of the study, were related to our participants' production of symbol combinations. We found that, when we compared their performance on these measures with whether they produced symbol combinations, there was no significant relationship.

Influence of Partner Combinations One explanation for the emergence of combinations was that participants were imitating the symbol-combination input they received from their adult partners. We analyzed the composition of the partners' lexigram combinations as well as the extent of similarity between partner lexigram combinations and participant combinations. Although the partners of Combiners modeled a variety of combinations, they did not consistently repeat phrases as models for the Combiners,

Table 5.7. Patterns of predominant semantic relations expressed in early spoken combinations

Pattern	Function
1	To draw attention to something, identify something, or assign class membership
2	To remark on specific properties of objects
3	To express possession
4	To express plurality or iteration
5	To express recurrence or alternate exemplars of a type
6	To note disappearance of objects
7	To express negation
8	To express actor-action relations
9	To note location and movement
10	To request
11	None of the above

Adapted from Braine (1976). Reprinted with minor revisions from Wilkinson, K.M., Romski, M.A., & Sevcik, R.A. (1994). Emergence of visual-graphic symbol combinations by youth with moderate or severe mental retardation. *Journal of Speech and Hearing Research, 37,* 887; reprinted by permission.

and their combinations did not differ from those of the partners of the Noncombiners.

Implications of These Research Findings Thus, the findings suggest that the symbol input of the adult partners was not responsible for the emergence of symbol combinations in the participants. These findings are important for two reasons. First, they suggest that the participants' symbol-combination patterns may resemble the early developmental patterns of speaking children and were not a result of mere rote imitation. Second, these findings suggest that the inclusion of symbols that promote symbol combinations in the vocabulary is extremely important for facilitating language development. Advancing individuals from single-symbol use to symbol combinations permits them to convey more complex information to their partners in an increased variety of environments and to function more fully and independently in society.

Role of Medical Etiology in SAL Use

In this section, we briefly address the role of the participant's medical etiology in SAL use. We have often been asked whether there were differences in our participants' SAL use based on their medical etiologies. Of particular interest has been the performance of participants with Down syndrome compared with participants with autism and mental retardation. We assume that the interest in these populations comes from the distinct language development literatures that exist about them. Individuals with Down syndrome usually develop speech (Mervis, 1988; Miller, 1992), although there are reports of individuals who do not speak (B. Hart, personal communication, October 1993; Miller, 1992). Speaking children with autism and mental retardation usually encounter considerable difficulty with the social use of language (Prizant & Wetherby, 1987; Tager-Flusberg, 1988). In contrast, some individuals with autism and mental retardation do not speak at all. Very little is known about their potential language development.

As described in Chapter 3, the number of our participants with each medical etiology was small. Two participants had a medical etiology of Down syndrome (DE and KW), and two were identified with autism and mental retardation through their school psychological records (EC and MH). With our colleague Robinson (Romski, Sevcik, & Robinson, 1992), we examined the communicative use skills of these four participants in order to determine similarities and differences in their SAL use patterns. We used a subset of our language transcript database from the second year of the study for this examination.

SAL Use Patterns In our sampling, EC and MH, the two participants with autism and mental retardation, produced 494 and 1,180 utterances, respectively. The two participants with Down syndrome, DE and KW, produced 936 and 1,103 utterances, respectively.

The majority of these four participants' communications were responses to the communications of others. The SAL was the primary means for communication by the four, with the exception of MH, whose primary means were vocalizations followed by the SAL. The pragmatic functions of the participants' communications (i.e., initiation, response) are depicted in Figure 5.5. Initiations served primarily to direct the attention of the partner, with the exception of DE's initiations, which were used for a variety of functions. The participants' responses spanned the range of communicative functions.

This analysis of the four participants' SAL use revealed a greater degree of similarity between the communicative use patterns of the two participants with autism and mental retardation and the two participants with Down syndrome than might have been expected, given the distinct literatures on spoken language development in these two groups. It is important to note that EC and MH, the participants with autism and mental retardation, gave us the impression that they were more interested in the mechanical operation of the speech-output device itself than in using it to communicate. Perhaps, in general, the participants' comparable degrees of cognitive impairment and their use of the SAL for communication overrode any differences that etiology may have produced. The small number of participants with each etiology, along with individual differences in communicative use, suggest, however, that these findings should be viewed very cautiously.

DIRECTIONS FOR PRACTICE

What can practice take from the communicative use findings reported in this chapter? There are six broad directions for practice that emerged from our findings about communicative use. These directions are 1) the utility of naturalistic language experiences, 2) the use of speech-output communication devices, 3) the integration of SAL use into natural communicative repertoires, 4) the role of the lexicon in augmented communication development, 5) the use of augmented input by communicative partners, and 6) the importance of including peers in social interactions. Although each of these directions is discussed separately in the following pages, it is important to point out that they are best integrated into practice as a set.

Utility of Naturalistic Language Intervention Experiences

The SAL clearly augmented, in the truest sense of the word, our participants' communications. It provided a conventional way to convey specific information and interact with adults and peers in a variety of daily home and school contexts. The ability to communicate effectively through the SAL provided a pathway by which our participants were able to enter into the social world of symbolic communication and master initial language skills during *natural* experiences. These language experiences provided a highly functional approach for teaching communication and language skills to individuals with severe communication disabilities. Using this approach, the focus for practice is on structuring and exploiting communicative opportunities that occur typically. To do this, the practitioner must engineer the environment so that the child has access to communication (e.g., the MegaWOLF communication device), a functional vocabulary, and partners who are informed about the child's means of communication and how to facilitate further development. To successfully and continually create such an environment is no small accomplishment and requires a flexible service delivery model.

Use of Speech-Output Communication Devices

Practitioners typically do not select a speech-output communication device as the medium for language learning for consumers. In the past, manual sign systems and cardboard communication boards have been the choice for physically typical youth with significant mental retardation. With the tremendous increase in the availability of speech-output communication devices specifically targeted to this population (e.g., MegaWOLF, MacCaw), this practice is beginning to change.

The speech-output feature of the SAL permitted our participants to compensate for having to use a visual communication system by automatically linking their visual communication with the familiar auditory and spoken modality in social interactional contexts. It provided the participants with a multimodal system of communication that included a voice yet retained the visual modality that was helpful to the participants.

The auditory signal also permitted partners to hear the speech feedback produced when a symbol was activated and to immediately comprehend the communication. This feature is particularly

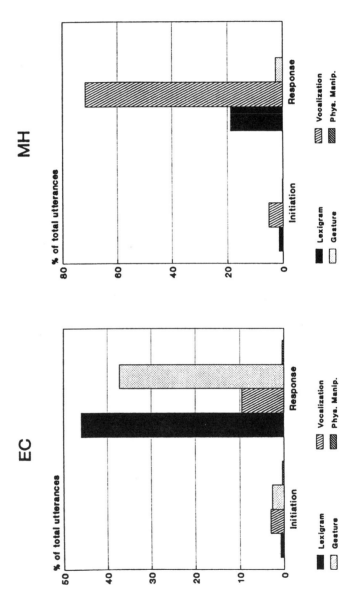

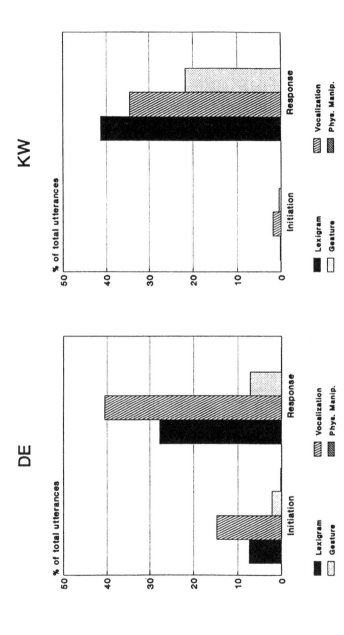

Figure 5.5. Type of communication (initiations and responses) by mode of communication (lexigram, gesture, vocalization, physical manipulation) of MH's, EC's, DE's, and KW's communications. Lexigram = SAL use; Gesture, vocalization, physical manipulation = Non-SAL use.

109

important when youth are functioning in the general community and interacting with unfamiliar communicative partners. The use of speech-output communication devices as the medium for language learning can allow youth with little or no functional speech to follow a course of language development that is similar to that of youth who speak because they too can speak—by computerized means. With the expanded capabilities and availability of reasonably priced speech-output communication devices, their use by individuals with severe mental retardation is finally moving beyond the realm of research and into the domain of recommended practice.

Integration of SAL Use into Natural Communicative Repertoires

For the participants we studied, vocalizations were a robust form; they continued to constitute a high proportion of their communications even after extensive SAL experience. Most of our participants who vocalized, even if unintelligibly, produced forms that marked communicative turns and were interpreted as serving a communicative function. Symbol use emerged and was maintained in the context of these vocal communication skills. Vocal forms apparently provided a familiar support for the participants' symbol usage. Neither the vocal form nor the visual symbol was dominant in their communications. Instead, communicative function and participant history and experience were equally important factors in how symbols and vocalizations were used in conversational exchanges. In addition, vocalizations did not decrease with SAL use. In fact, they increased (see Chapter 6 on word production skills), thus affirming that the use of an augmented language system does not diminish or inhibit an individual's desire or ability to vocalize or to speak.

Role of the Lexicon in Augmented Language Development

Another important consideration for practice is the type and size of the lexicon available to individuals. The lexicon available to our participants helped shape their social interactions as well as the content and complexity of their communications. The use of a broad range of symbols likely influences an individual's ability to engage in communication with multiple partners in varied social contexts and influences the partner's perception of the youth's social competence.

Youth like our participants hear many more words spoken in context than they can produce. Production of words is dependent on the oral-motor abilities of the speakers themselves. Although individuals with little or no functional speech are often exposed to a spoken input vocabulary comparable to that of a speaking child, their production is usually constrained by the number of visual-graphic symbol vocabulary items available on their communication systems. A wide range of vocabulary items, including different word types, that are updated and changed as needed for specific activities and between environments can greatly facilitate vocabulary learning. Although the SAL addressed transitional activities by building vocabulary to be used both within and between environments, there are some basic limits on vocabulary access that practice must acknowledge. The symbols individuals use are drawn from the lexicon that is made available to them by the practitioners and their families. Their ability to regulate interpersonal exchanges using culturally appropriate ways of communicating is greatly enhanced if they have access to a lexicon that meets their needs.

Use of Augmented Input by Communicative Partners

Another consideration for practice is the use of augmented input by partners in the intervention process. The influence of the linguistic environment has frequently been overlooked with respect to augmented language development. Individuals like our participants typically do not have opportunities to observe the use of their communication devices by others. Partner use of augmented input provides a model of augmented language use and can also serve as an important reinforcer for the user. Because all of the communicative partners communicate by using the system, it is an implicit statement that the augmented language system is an acceptable form of communication.

Importance of Including Peers in Social Interactions

One striking observation from our research was that our participants, overall, communicated very little with their peers. Given the educational focus of inclusion, this is certainly an area that is essential to successful communication intervention. Not only are opportunities to communicate and interact with peers needed, but the lexicon provided for the augmented user must also allow typical age-appropriate exchanges. The topics, the phrasing, and the words themselves must be conducive to exchanges between friends and classmates about familiar people, places, items, and events.

REFERENCES

Adamson, L.B., Romski, M.A., Deffebach, K.P., & Sevcik, R.A. (1992). Symbol vocabulary and the focus of conversations: Augmenting language development for youth with mental retardation. *Journal of Speech and Hearing Research, 35,* 1333–1344.

Braine, M.D.S. (1976). Children's first word combinations. *Monographs of the Society for Research in Child Development, 41*(1, Serial No. 164).

Carrier, J. (1974). Non-speech noun usage training with severely and profoundly retarded children. *Journal of Speech and Hearing Research, 17,* 510–512.

Goldstein, H., & Kaczmarek, L. (1991). Promoting communicative interaction among children in integrated intervention settings. In S. Warren & J. Reichle (Eds.), *Communication and language intervention series: Vol. 1. Causes and effects in communication and language intervention* (pp. 81–111). Baltimore: Paul H. Brookes Publishing Co.

Greenfield, P.M., & Savage-Rumbaugh, S. (1990). Grammatical combination in *Pan paniscus:* Processes of learning and invention in the evolution and development of language. In S.T. Parker & K.R. Gibson (Eds.), *Language and intelligence in monkeys and apes: Comparative developmental perspectives* (pp. 540–578). New York: Cambridge University Press.

Hunt, P., Alwell, M., & Goetz, L. (1991). Interacting with peers through conversational turntaking with a communication book adaptation. *Augmentative and Alternative Communication, 7,* 117–126.

Karlan, G.R., Brenn-White, B., Lentz, A., Hodur, P., Egger, D., & Frankoff, D. (1982). Establishing generalized productive verb-noun phrase usage in a manual language system with moderately handicapped children. *Journal of Speech and Hearing Disorders, 47,* 31–42.

Knopp, C.B., & Recchia, S.L. (1990). The issues of multiple pathways in the development of handicapped children. In R.M. Hodapp, J.A. Burack, & E. Zigler (Eds.), *Issues in the developmental approach to mental retardation* (pp. 272–293). New York: Cambridge University Press.

Mervis, C.B. (1988). Early lexical development: Theory and application. In L. Nadel (Ed.), *The psychobiology of Down syndrome* (pp. 101–143). Cambridge, MA: Bradford/MIT Press.

Miller, J. (1992). Lexical development in young children with Down syndrome. In R.S. Chapman (Ed.), *Processes in language acquisition and disorders* (pp. 202–216). St Louis, MO: Mosby-Yearbook.

Miller, J., & Chapman, R. (1985). *Systematic analysis of language transcripts (SALT)* [Computer program]. Madison: University of Wisconsin.

Prizant, B.M., & Wetherby, A.M. (1987). Communicative intent: A framework for understanding social-communicative behavior in autism. *Journal of the American Academy of Child and Adolescent Psychiatry, 26,* 472–479.

Reichle, J., York, J., & Sigafoos, J. (1991). *Implementing augmentative and alternative communication: Strategies for learners with severe disabilities.* Baltimore: Paul H. Brookes Publishing Co.

Romski, M.A., & Sevcik, R.A. (1988). Augmentative and alternative communication: Considerations for individuals with severe intellectual disabilities. *Augmentative and Alternative Communication, 4,* 83–93.

Romski, M.A., Sevcik, R.A., Reumann, R., & Pate, J.L. (1989). Youngsters with moderate or severe retardation and severe spoken language impairments I: Extant communicative patterns. *Journal of Speech and Hearing Disorders, 54,* 366–373.

Romski, M.A., Sevcik, R.A., & Robinson, B. (1992). Social communication patterns of augmented language learners with mental retardation and autism [Abstract]. *Proceedings of the 25th Annual Gatlinburg Conference on Research and Theory in Mental Retardation and Developmental Disabilities,* Gatlinburg, TN, p. 147.

Romski, M.A., Sevcik, R.A., Robinson, B., & Bakeman, R. (1994). Adult-directed communications of youth with mental retardation using the System for Augmenting Language. *Journal of Speech and Hearing Research, 37,* 617–628.

Romski, M.A., Sevcik, R.A., & Wilkinson, K.M. (1994). Peer-directed communicative interactions of augmented language learners with mental retardation. *American Journal on Mental Retardation, 98,* 527–538.

Sevcik, R.A., Romski, M.A., Watkins, R., & Deffebach, K. (1995). Adult partner-augmented communication input to youth with mental retardation using the System for Augmenting Language (SAL). *Journal of Speech and Hearing Research, 38,* 902–912.

Sevcik, R.A., Savage-Rumbaugh, E.S., & Rumbaugh, D.M. (1996). *A comprehensive analysis of graphic symbol acquisition and use: Evidence from an infant bonobo (Pan paniscus).* Manuscript submitted for publication.

Tager-Flusberg, H. (1988). On the nature of a language acquisition disorder: The example of autism. In F. Kessel (Ed.), *The development of language and language researchers: Essays in honor of Roger Brown* (pp. 249–267). Hillsdale, NJ: Lawrence Erlbaum Associates.

Wilkinson, K.M., Romski, M.A., & Sevcik, R.A. (1994). Emergence of visual-graphic symbol combinations by youth with moderate or severe mental retardation. *Journal of Speech and Hearing Research, 37,* 883–895.

Chapter 6

Language and Communicative Achievements

Vocabulary Mastery and Resulting Gains

Chapter 5 provided an overview of how our participants employed the System for Augmenting Language (SAL) in order to communicate in everyday interactions. When an intervention consists of arranging the natural environment to promote communication, communicative use is just one dimension of what the participants learned as they gained experience with the SAL. Another dimension in which achievement could be assessed is vocabulary mastery, specifically the participants' comprehension and production of the symbols they were using apart from the contextual framework in which they used them. It is difficult to systematically assess what a participant knows about the symbols he is using within the context of use, because aspects of the natural context (e.g., gestures, facial expressions, routines) may actually be supporting their use and serve to confound the assessment process. As with typically developing children, initial word use may be tied to the routine contexts in which it occurs (Bruner, 1983). For example, FG was able to use the symbol CEREAL, which always appeared on his display panel in the same position, to request cereal for the daily breakfast at school. When faced with a color photograph of a bowl of cereal and the cereal box in a structured situation and asked, "What is this?," he was initially unable to choose the symbol for

CEREAL from three other lexigrams in the randomly ordered array. The confrontational forced-choice naming task required a different level of understanding than was necessary in the context of the interaction. Assessing what the participants learned about the symbols they used permitted us to identify patterns of how they were abstracting symbol meaning from the natural instructional context.

As discussed in Chapter 4, across the longitudinal investigation, we systematically collected information about the participants' patterns of vocabulary knowledge five times (every other month) during each of the 2 school years by using the Vocabulary Assessment Measures (VAMs). The VAM Probes included assessments of symbol comprehension and production as well as measures of the participants' word production and printed English word recognition skills. (See Chapter 4 for a detailed review of VAM procedures.) In this chapter, we focus on the participants' vocabulary mastery. First, we describe accomplishments in vocabulary comprehension and production. Next, we present some noteworthy findings about the strategies our participants employed to master new vocabulary. Then, we discuss some findings about speech production and printed word recognition. Finally, we provide examples of how a symbol vocabulary gives us a window into our participants' knowledge base.

Accomplishments in Vocabulary Comprehension and Production

As indicated in Chapter 4, the participants had two types of vocabulary on their display panels: referential symbols and social-regulative symbols. Referential symbols represented concrete items, including objects, foods, and locations. Social-regulative symbols referred to functions focused on the speaker, the partner, or the communicative link between them.

Referential Symbols We (Romski & Sevcik, 1994) examined the patterns of referential vocabulary acquisition evidenced by our participants. In order to assess referential symbol knowledge, we used the VAMs' structured task format and 35 mm photographs of the referents as the stimuli. Prior to the investigation, we had assessed the participants' knowledge of the first 12 referential symbols that would appear on their displays. None of the participants could identify the symbols for the 12 items, although some participants comprehended the spoken words for the symbols.

We employed two approaches in order to examine our participants' referential symbol learning over time. First, we examined the accuracy of referential symbol use on each VAM assessment across the 2 years of the study. Second, we inspected the consistency of their VAM comprehension and production performance for individual words across time.

Accuracy of Performance For each participant's vocabulary, we tallied the percentage of symbols correctly identified in the VAM comprehension and production tasks. We used a percentage measure because the total number of referential vocabulary items on an individual display varied across participants and time. During the study's first year, the number ranged from a minimum of 1 to a maximum of 18; during Year 2, the number of referential items on the display ranged from a minimum of 12 to a maximum of 25.

As can be seen in Figure 6.1, mean comprehension scores (range across participants = 0%–100%, average across probes = 78%) remained fairly consistent across the study's 2 years, with one exception. There was a fairly deep dip in comprehension performance at VAM Probe 9. During this period of time, nine of the participants' vocabularies expanded to include, at minimum, seven new referential symbols. Production performance was consistently poorer (range across participants = 0%–100%, average across probes = 66%) than comprehension performance, except at the last probe of the first school year (Probe 5). At Probe 5, production performance was comparable to comprehension performance. At

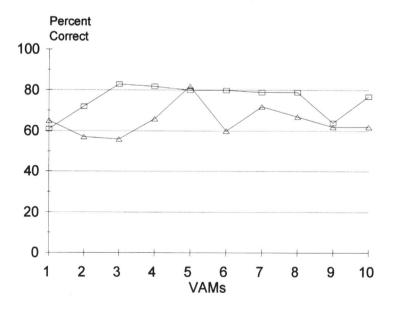

Figure 6.1. Mean VAM comprehension and production scores (in percent) for referential symbols across the study's 2 years. (–⊟– = comprehension, –△– = production.)

the beginning of Year 2 (Probe 6), however, there was a fairly large and significant decrement in production performance (from 82% to 60%). In contrast, comprehension performance remained consistent from the end of Year 1 (80%) to the beginning of Year 2 (80%).

Consistency of Performance For each referential symbol assessed, we also identified four possible outcomes, which are listed in Table 6.1. These outcomes describe the relationship between individual participant's vocabulary performance in comprehension and production. Figure 6.2 illustrates the proportion of referential vocabulary items that fell into each of the four outcomes collapsed across Years 1 and 2. As can be seen, the largest percentage of the vocabulary across Year 1 (VAMs 1–5, mean = 54%, range = 38%–71%) and Year 2 (VAMs 6–10, mean = 45%, range = 39%–48%) was both comprehended and produced by participants. The next most frequent vocabulary outcomes across Years 1 and 2 were Outcome 2, comprehension only (Year 1: VAMs 1–5, mean = 33%, range = 8%–24%; Year 2: VAMs 6–10, mean = 22%, range = 17%–25%), and Outcome 4, neither comprehending nor producing the symbol (Year 1: VAMs 1–5, mean = 22%, range = 12%–31%; Year 2: VAMs 6–10, mean = 25%, range = 21%–28%). Production-only performance remained consistently low across the 2 years (Year 1: VAMs 1–5, mean = 7%, range = 5%–12%; Year 2: VAMs 6–10, mean = 7%, range = 4%–9%).

Social-Regulative Symbols The participants' knowledge of social-regulative symbols was more difficult for us to assess because the meanings of the symbols were not easily depicted by 35 mm photographs (e.g., PLEASE). Because of this difficulty, we altered our assessment procedure for social-regulative symbols. As a baseline measure, we asked parents and teachers to complete a brief questionnaire about their perceptions of the participants' knowledge of social-regulative words. In general, parents and teachers reported that the participants had some knowledge of these words in context. Next, we used VAM production tasks to measure the participants' knowledge about social-regulative symbols because of the difficulty in illustrating the social-regulative vocabulary. It should be remembered that social-regulative sym-

Table 6.1.   Possible VAM comprehension and production outcomes

1. The participant comprehended and produced the symbol.
2. The participant comprehended but did not produce the symbol.
3. The participant produced but did not comprehend the symbol.
4. The participant neither comprehended nor produced the symbol.

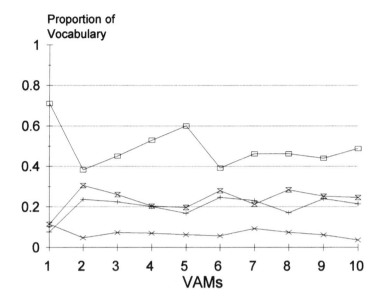

Figure 6.2. Proportion of referential vocabulary for the four VAM comprehension and production outcomes across the study's 2 years. (—𝔁— = symbol neither comprehended nor produced; —+— = symbol comprehended but not produced; —✗— = symbol produced but not comprehended; —◻— = symbol comprehended and produced.)

bols were not introduced until the end of Year 1, so information is presented for Year 2 only (VAMs 6–10) about knowledge of these symbols. Figure 6.3 illustrates the mean production scores for social-regulative symbols (range across participants 0%–100%, average across probes = 37%) were fairly consistent across Year 2. Production performance on these symbols was consistently lower than on the referential symbols.

Overall Symbol Performance We found that referential symbols were correctly identified and maintained by our participants, although comprehension performance was consistently greater than production performance. In addition, participants were more likely to identify a symbol in comprehension and production than in either comprehension or production alone.

Referential symbol knowledge was generally better than social-regulative symbol knowledge, although a direct comparison is not possible, given the differences in assessment strategies. Nevertheless, the social-regulative symbols served to broaden the focus of conversations (see Chapter 5 and Adamson, Romski, Deffebach, & Sevcik, 1992, for a discussion of this issue).

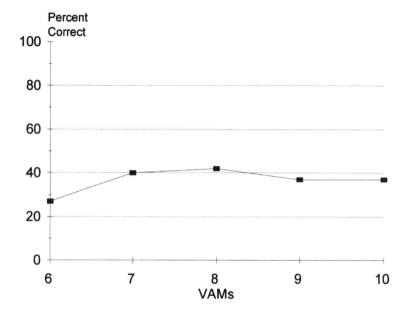

Figure 6.3. Mean production scores for social-regulative symbols across Year 2.

Accounting for Symbol Learning

Overall, our participants demonstrated a wide range of vocabulary performance across the study's 2 years. Some participants learned quickly, while others learned more slowly. Although these participants were chosen because they had little or no productive oral language skills, as discussed, they varied on other skills such as speech comprehension.

Child-language researchers have argued that lexical acquisition proceeds rapidly in the typically developing child because the child has a set of operating principles that guide the learning of words (e.g., Golinkoff, Mervis, & Hirsh-Pasek, 1994; Mervis & Bertrand, 1993, 1994). One of the more advanced principles that directs the child's learning is the Novel Name–Nameless Category (N3C) principle (Golinkoff et al., 1994). This principle holds that when a child hears a novel word in the presence of an unknown object, he or she will immediately map the novel name onto the novel (nameless) entity. The N3C principle, then, enables the young, typically developing child to map the meanings of new words at a rapid rate and with very little exposure to the new words. The behavioral demonstration of the N3C principle is known as *fast mapping*.

We were interested in determining if and how our participants used this principle to learn symbol meanings. In a follow-up study with our colleagues Robinson, Mervis, and Bertrand (Romski, Sevcik, Robinson, Mervis, & Bertrand, 1996), we assessed to what extent our participants acquired new symbols on first exposure to novel spoken words+symbols. We adapted procedures developed by Mervis and Bertrand (1994) in order to assess our participants' abilities to learn novel symbols when first exposed to them. We presented participants with sets of four known words+symbols and one unknown word+symbol and asked them to identify the novel one. To ensure that none of the participants had been exposed to these novel words+symbols, we gave the novel words+symbols nonsense names such as "gegot" and "wiztor."

After one exposure to these novel words+symbols, seven participants (DC, DE, EC, JA, KW, MH, and TE) were able to choose the novel object that represented the nonsense word+symbol. The remaining five participants were not able to choose the novel objects.

We then conducted three assessments: immediately following the participants' initial experience, as well as 1 day and 15 days after the original exposure. In these assessments, we measured both comprehension and production of the nonsense words+symbols. It is important to note that in these assessments a distractor stimulus (another novel but unnamed object) was included to ensure that the participants had not simply selected the novel or unknown object. The seven Mappers, as we called them, retained comprehension of at least two of the four novel words+symbols for periods of more than 2 weeks with no intervening experience. The Mappers also generalized their comprehension knowledge to production performance. The Non-Mappers did not retain any word+symbol knowledge in comprehension or production.

More than half of our participants were able to rapidly map, retain, and generalize the names of novel words+symbols, even though they had little exposure to them and no intervening naturalistic communicative experience with them. In fact, more than 3 months after the study was completed, JA demonstrated that he still retained his knowledge of one novel word+symbol. At that time, JA was being assessed for a new speech-output communication device with an alphanumeric keyboard and an LED screen. While he was exploring the new device, he was observed to type out "witzor" (incorrect spelling of "wiztor"), one of the nonsense words from the study. The investigator conducting the assessment, amazed at what JA had typed, retrieved the objects from the study and showed them to him. JA correctly identified the object labeled as "wiztor."

Some of the participants, then, readily learned to comprehend and produce symbols by using the N3C lexical principle. These findings suggest that the use of this principle is one explanation of how our participants learned to use symbols through exposure to them. The participants who were not Mappers, however, also learned to use symbols during natural communicative exchanges. In Chapter 7, we discuss some patterns of symbol achievement that emerged and relate them to distinct learning strategies.

Other Vocabulary-Related Achievements

In addition to learning the meanings of the symbols that were on the symbol displays, two particular skills that have been reported to emerge as a consequence of augmented language interventions are worthy of discussion. The first, a highly coveted achievement, is the production of intelligible spoken words. The second skill, sight word recognition, is equally important to an individual's educational development because it can serve as a building block for the development of reading skills (Koppenhaver, Coleman, Kalman, & Yoder, 1991). It is important to note that when we began our longitudinal study, we *did not* intend to teach the participants to speak or to read. However, we did intend to measure the incidental learning of these two important and often discussed skills.

Production of Intelligible Spoken Words It is generally accepted by practitioners that augmented language experiences, such as manual signs, communication boards, and speech-output communication devices, support and do not hinder spoken language development (Beukelman & Mirenda, 1992). Unfortunately, there are only a few empirical studies to support this clinical observation (e.g., Fulwiler & Fouts, 1976; Kouri, 1988; Miller & Miller, 1973; Romski, Sevcik, & Pate, 1988; Yoder & Layton, 1988). In our own earlier work, for example, we (Romski, Sevcik, & Pate, 1988) reported a consistent improvement in the word approximation skills of a young woman with severe mental retardation and dysarthria (dysfunction of the articulators due to paralysis), as well as the emergence of two conventional spoken words, "apple" /aepl/ and "Debbie" /dɛbi/, for symbols that were on her communication display. Our assessment of her speech production skills before and after her experience with visual-graphic symbols in a structured communicative context revealed that, by the time she had acquired 20 symbols, not only did she produce these two words, but also all of her other 18 production attempts changed from single syllables to include bisyllabic consonant-vowel-consonant-vowel utterances. In a study of 60 children with autism, Yoder and Layton (1988) reported that baseline vocal imitation skills were the best predictor of speech production associated with manual sign language instruction. In addition, pre-intervention age and IQ level also contributed to spoken language development.

Early on in this study, we began to observe, and parents and teachers began to report, changes in individual participants' speech intelligibility. These reports continued across the course of our investigation. During the first CUP observation after introduction of the SAL, DE's mother reported, "He never had said 'ice cream' before and now he says 'ice cream' like the Votrax system says it." At the end of the study's first year, a visitor to the Language Research Center (LRC), a prominent scholar in augmentative communication, questioned why we had included TE in our study. Our visitor remarked, "He talks." The words that TE was producing were words on his SAL display. We showed our visitor baseline videotapes of TE to illustrate that he had not produced intelligible words prior to the onset of his SAL use. These observations and others suggested to us that we might be able to identify specific changes in our participants' abilities to produce speech.

Assessing Changes in Speech Production Measuring speech intelligibility has traditionally been considered with respect to adult speakers with dysarthria. Kent, Weismer, Kent, and Rosenbek (1989) have argued that tests of speech intelligibility require a precise delineation of the purpose and conditions under which the data are collected if they are to provide a valid measurement of speech intelligibility. However, how does one assess changes in an individual's ability to produce speech if he has never before produced speech? One approach would be to document the onset of vocalization. As shown in Table 3.4, however, the majority of our participants were attempting to vocalize at the beginning of the study, although their vocalizations were rated as unintelligible. Their vocalizations were most probably unintelligible because their speech mechanisms did not function in a sufficiently mobile manner for intelligible speech (see Table 3.6). Thus, we chose to document changes in the intelligibility of the vocalizations that participants produced.

Our purpose for examining intelligibility was twofold. First, we wanted to describe the *emergence* of spoken words in youth who previously had severely restricted vocal repertoires. Second, we wanted to identify the factors that may have contributed to these emerging abilities. We limited our assessment to single words because we observed no evidence of extant connected speech in our participants. Another difference between assessing our participants and adults with dysarthria is that we were interested in improvements in single-word production skills associated with the use of augmented language experience specifically via speech-output communication devices. Thus, we measured the intelligibility of words that were represented on the participants' SAL displays.

Improvements in Speech Intelligibility In collaboration with our colleagues Robinson and Wilkinson (Romski, Sevcik, Robinson, & Wilkinson, 1990), we used the participants' performances on the VAM speech production task as our data set. In this task, participants were presented with 35 mm photographs depicting each vocabulary item on their display panel and asked, "What is this?" (see Table 4.8). Spontaneous vocal responses were recorded on audiotape. If the participant did not respond within 10 seconds, a vocal model was provided and the participant was asked to imitate the model; for example, "Hotdog, say 'hotdog'." Because we thought the changes in speech intelligibility were fairly subtle, we made comparisons between the participants' performance at three points: baseline, the end of the first school year, and the end of the second school year. All vocal samples, with and without a model, were spliced onto audiotapes in a random order to ensure that judgments were objective and not influenced by the order in which they were presented.

An independent speech-language pathologist who did not know the purpose of our investigation rated the randomly ordered word-production samples on the audiotapes using the Intelligibility Rating Scale (IRS) (Romski, Plenge, & Sevcik, 1988). The IRS (see Table 3.5) is an 8-point rating scale developed specifically to provide a conservative rating of single-word intelligibility. Ratings ranged from 1 for undifferentiated vocalizations to 7 for completely intelligible words, with 0 for no response. To provide a measure of interlistener agreement, a second speech-language pathologist rated a small portion (15%) of the word samples and produced ratings that agreed with the first speech-language pathologist's ratings on 95% of the word samples.

Seven of the 13 participants (DC, EC, JA, KW, MH, TE, and TF) increased the proportion of words that were rated intelligible. Prior to the onset of SAL use, the median rating of intelligibility in the spontaneous or no-model condition was 1.75 (range = 1.0–3.0). These ratings meant that, in general, our participants produced differentiated vocalizations. After 1 and 2 years of SAL experience, the median intelligibility rating increased to 2.0 (range = 1.0–4.0) and 2.5 (range = 1.0–5.0), respectively. It is also notable that the range of ratings broadened from a low of *undifferentiated vocalizations* to a high of *unintelligible with correct syllabification* and then *intelligible with multiple articulation errors*. Table 6.2 provides examples of the change in the phonetic makeup of individual words for TE from baseline to Year 1 and then to Year 2.

Factors Contributing to Speech Improvement Given the vocal histories of our participants and their severely limited vocal repertoires, these modest increases in speech intelligibility were significant because they suggested that the participants' vocal abilities were changing. What factors may have contributed to these increases? We assessed the relationship between improvement in speech intelligibility and the two vocal imitation skill measures discussed in Chapter 3: 1) the vocal imitation scale (Scale IIIA of the Ordinal Scales of Psychological Development [Uzgiris & Hunt, 1975]) and 2) the intelligibility ratings from our baseline VAMs in which a spoken word was modeled. Scores on these assessments were not significantly related to improvement in speech intelligibility, which indicated that our participants' improvements were not due to vocal imitation abilities. Although these findings differ from those of Yoder and Layton (1988), who found that vocal imitation skills did predict improvement in speech production, there were other differences between the two studies as well. Our participants were chronologically older and had diagnoses of more significant mental retardation, and our speech measures were different from those of Yoder and Layton (1988).

We thought that another factor that may have contributed to improved speech intelligibility was the speech-output communication device itself. It provided the participant with a consistent model of the spoken word in a synthesized form immediately following each symbol usage. To assess this contribution, we measured the rate of symbol usage and correlated it with our participants' improvements in speech intelligibility. Again, we found no significant relationship.

Table 6.2. Examples of changes in the phonetic makeup of spoken words in TE's symbol vocabulary

Word	Baseline	Year 1	Year 2
Ice cream	/aɪsɑ/	/aɪsi/	/aɪs kri/
Plate	/spe/	/pet/	/ples/
Record player	/rɛkə/	/rɛkə/	/wekaəpe/

Still another explanation is suggested by one participant's imitation of the synthetic speech signal. Recall that DE's mother observed that he imitated the Votrax synthesizer. It may be that it is not the quantity of feedback the participants received, but the change in the type of signal that the participants were hearing that was a factor in improved speech intelligibility. The Votrax voice is distinctly different from natural speech. Each time a participant touched a symbol, the computer provided a consistent signal at a slowed rate without intonation. This distinct sound may have helped the youth to parse the speech stream in a way that had not been previously available to him. The synthesized speech signal was not affected by contextual speech cues.

Our findings provide data-based evidence for the emergence of intelligible speech as participants had SAL experience. Although we have not been able to specify the exact factor(s) that permitted our participants to develop their vocal repertoires, we suspect that the speech-output device provided them with a consistent model of the spoken word in a synthesized form immediately following each symbol usage, and this remains a possible reason for the changes in speech intelligibility.

Recognizing Printed English Words Literacy skills are also related to augmented language learning. The majority of youth with significant mental retardation encounter considerable difficulty learning to read (Singh & Singh, 1986; Zigler & Hodapp, 1986). Given its widespread utility, the ability to recognize print had obvious social and communicative advantages for our participants.

To date, there are few studies on reading skills of nonspeaking individuals with mental retardation. In the early 1970s, Sidman (Sidman, 1970; Sidman & Cresson, 1973) reported the successful use of a mediated-transfer paradigm as one approach by which to establish simple reading skills for two speaking young adults with severe mental retardation. Kuntz and colleagues (Kuntz, Carrier, & Hollis, 1978) reported that 14 adolescents with severe mental retardation who learned traditional orthographic words after experience with abstract nonorthographic plastic symbols required fewer trials than did other adolescents who had had comparable experience with pictographs. It is important to note that the nonorthographic symbols used in this study were abstract and did not resemble the referents or the meanings the referents conveyed.

The belief that oral language skills not only buttress but also are requisite to the development of reading skills has presented a specific challenge for individuals such as our participants who have not developed adequate oral language skills (Koppenhaver,

Coleman, Kalman, & Yoder, 1991). Some of our participants had previous experience with reading programs as part of their IEPs. Teachers and parents reported that they did not make significant progress, and reading goals were subsequently omitted from their IEPs. Because we paired the printed English word with each symbol by placing it above the symbol (see Figure 2.1), we were interested in determining whether any participants learned the meanings of the printed English words.

Together with our colleague Robinson (Sevcik, Romski, & Robinson, 1991), we used the VAMs pooled across baseline, Year 1, and Year 2 to examine the printed English word recognition for each participant's referential and social-regulative vocabulary independent of the symbol. Our baseline VAMs indicated that EC, MH, and JA consistently recognized the majority of these printed words and maintained their skill across the 2 years of the study. Of the remaining 10 participants, we found that 6 (BB, DC, DE, JL, TF, and TE) demonstrated an increase in the recognition of referential words from baseline through Probes 5 and 10 (mean = 34%, 45%, 77%, respectively) and for social-regulative words from baseline (which was actually Probe 5) (mean = 28%) to Probe 10 (mean = 49%). BB, DE, and JL's increases were more dramatic from Probe 5 to Probe 10 for referential words. Perhaps they required additional SAL experience in order to begin to pair the printed English words with the symbols.

Some participants learned to recognize both referential and social-regulative printed words during the course of SAL experience, even though they did not receive any explicit instruction concerning the relationships between the symbols and their printed word equivalents during the course of the study. These findings demonstrate that some of our participants were able to independently extract some printed words from the stream of communicative information available to them. They are also consistent with the findings of Ehri and Roberts (1979), who found that typically developing beginning readers learned words better in the context of sentences than in an isolated word drill. The participants' age and previous unsuccessful experience in traditional classroom introductory reading programs seemed to suggest that they could not learn to recognize printed words. Traditionally, youth with cognitive and language disabilities are presented with a series of tasks that comprise what are believed to be the subskills of reading, for example, the discrimination of letters and sounds and the ability to visually scan from left to right. Our participants essentially bypassed these readiness skills and were confronted directly with whole words incorporated within meaningful communicative exchanges. As Gibson (1973) argued, meaning is an acquired association between a configuration of letters and the referent to be named. We made no attempt to draw upon or to enhance the discriminability of the printed words; they were always paired with their lexigram equivalent on the display. It remained the participant's task to make the association between the lexigram and the printed word. Thus, we strongly suspect that SAL experience played a role in this transfer of meaning.

Follow-Up Study Although these preliminary findings suggested that printed English word recognition is a byproduct of SAL experience, there were still unanswered questions about whether printed English words could be learned in the naturalistic context when lexigrams were *not* present. In a follow-up study, we compared the ability of four participants (JA, DC, EC, and DE) to learn novel lexigrams+printed English words and to learn novel printed English words for communication. Over a 10-week period of SAL experience, these four participants were given comparable access to a vocabulary display that depicted six unknown printed English words and six unknown lexigrams+printed English words. We randomly positioned the words and lexigrams on the 36-item SuperWOLF display.

Participants' comprehension and production of the lexigrams and printed English words were assessed at baseline and at the end of the 10-week period. Overall, these four participants comprehended (mean = 4.65) both of the visual forms better than they produced them (mean = 3.75). They also learned the printed English words alone slightly better than lexigrams+printed words (means = 4.75, 3.63, respectively). This finding is consistent with that of Kuntz and her colleagues (Kuntz et al., 1978) who suggested that, once an equivalency is established between graphic symbols and printed English words, meaning is readily attributed to the printed words.

Vocabulary as a Window Through Which to View Knowledge

The development of a visual-graphic symbol vocabulary has permitted some of our participants to reveal previously untapped psychological abilities through another research project that was a part of the LRC's grant. The Neuropsychological Foundations Project, led by Robin Morris, studied the relationships between brain function, language, and cognitive behaviors. We were able to use the participants' visual-graphic symbol vocabulary skills as the mode by which to assess a range of neuropsychological function, including attention and memory processes. In this section, we use two studies from this project to illustrate how the participants' working symbol vocabulary gave us a window into the knowledge and skills they possessed. The first study examined how visual-graphic symbol meanings may be differentially represented in the cortex when compared to nonmeaningful visual-graphic forms (Molfese, Morris, & Romski, 1990). The second study examined memory skills via the use of symbols and a computerized assessment system (Middleton, Sevcik, & Morris, 1993).

Brain–Behavior Relationships The first study focused on brain-behavior relationships. In this investigation, we employed a nonintrusive electrophysiological measure, known as auditory evoked potentials, to identify the locations or areas in the cortex of the brain where the participants' symbol knowledge may be processed.

In this study, Molfese et al. (1990) adapted a methodology (Molfese, 1989) previously employed with young, typically developing children who were just learning to talk. Six of our participants (DE, EC, FG, JL, KW, and TE) were shown known referential symbols from their vocabularies and symbols with which they had no experience. As they viewed each symbol, a series of auditory probe tones was simultaneously presented to evoke responses in the cortex. To record the auditory evoked responses (AERs), each of the participants had to wear electrodes placed on his scalp over the frontal, temporal, and parietal regions of the left and right hemispheres of the brain, as illustrated in Figure 6.4. The task required us to place the electrodes and leave them on for approximately 1 hour, and only six participants were able to tolerate this procedure. The other seven participants were judged not able to tolerate the electrode placement and thus were not included in this study.

The lexigram symbols to which the six participants had attached meaning were processed differently by the brain than lexigrams to which the participants had not attached meaning. The AER activity recorded from the left hemisphere frontal and temporal electrode sites successfully discriminated between the symbols that were individually meaningful and nonmeaningful to the six participants. In general, these findings suggest that the electrophysiological measures, when coupled with specific behavioral tasks, provide a unique opportunity to understand how individuals such as our participants process symbol meanings neurolinguistically.

Memory Processes The second study examined short-term memory of symbols (Middleton et al., 1993). Very little is actually known about the memory capacities of individuals such as our participants, because most measures of memory use verbal means

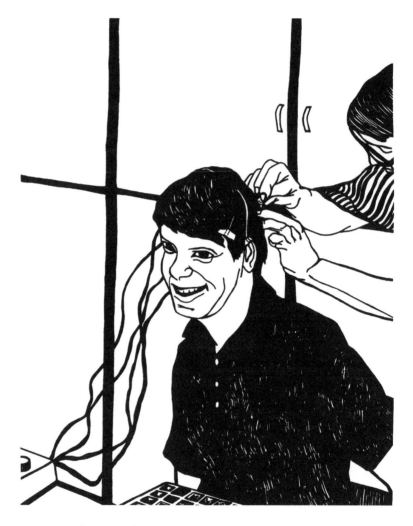

Figure 6.4.   Illustration of electrode placement in the study of brain–behavior relationships (Molfese, Morris, & Romski, 1990; illustration by Andrea Clay).

of assessment (e.g., Ellis, 1970). Bonta and Watters (1983), however, evaluated the role that use of American Sign Language played in the memory of children with developmental delays and spoken language impairments. Two children's recall performance improved when they used signs as mediators in a delayed memory task. This finding suggested that manual signs can function as a nonspeech mediator and can positively affect a child's performance on visual and auditory memory tasks.

Middleton et al. (1993) examined the short-term memory capabilities of three of our participants (JA, MH, and DC) who were able to pass a screening protocol for the computer-based task. Their known lexigram symbol vocabularies served as the stimuli. Using a computer-based match-to-sample task, the participants were asked to match target lexigrams in the presence of contrast lexigrams. First, the participant used a joystick to bring a cursor to a central location on the screen. The target lexigram then appeared on the monitor for 2 seconds. After a delay, varying from 1 second to 1 minute, a set of two lexigrams (one target, one contrast) appeared on the screen. The participant used the joystick to direct the cursor to his matching selection, which was recorded by the computer.

Target and contrast lexigrams were related to each other in one of four ways. One relationship was perceptual, in which the target and contrast lexigrams shared at least one geometric element. A second relationship was categorical, in which lexigrams were semantically related by category (e.g., FORK and KNIFE). In the third relationship, target and contrast lexigrams shared both perceptual and categorical elements, and in the fourth relationship, they shared neither.

The three participants remembered their symbols with as much as a 1-minute delay between the presentation of the target and contrast lexigram sets. The type of relationship between the target and contrast lexigrams, however, significantly influenced correct responses for MH and DC. The meaningfulness of the contrast lexigrams interfered with correct responses for one of the three participants.

These two studies are illustrations of how use of an augmented language system such as the SAL can serve as a window through which our participants' abilities can be examined. Without it, our participants' abilities may have been overlooked and/or underestimated. Use of the SAL permits us to investigate new areas of study (e.g., neurolinguistic processing, memory) that previously had not been possible, because our participants did not speak.

Directions for Practice

What can practice use from the vocabulary mastery findings we reported? There are three broad directions for practice that emerged from our findings about vocabulary mastery: 1) the importance of language comprehension skills, 2) the support for promoting spoken word production and printed word recognition skills, and 3) the use of consistent and systematic measurement tools.

Importance of Language Comprehension Skills One very important direction for practice is attention to the role of language comprehension in augmented language learning. When practitioners focus on augmented language learning, they typically highlight production or use skills. If we had not assessed comprehension skills as well, we would have presumed that a few of our participants were not making gains in augmented language learning.

Language comprehension has been the silent partner in augmented language acquisition and use (Romski & Sevcik, 1993). As with the process observed in typical and atypical children developing spoken language, augmented language intervention requires a blend of receptive and productive experiences. Although it is reasonable to place some emphasis on productive skills that permit an individual to effect a functional change in his environment, comprehension skills are an essential component in the development of the participant's other role as a *listener* in communicative exchanges. Functioning as a listener assumes an ability to comprehend symbols produced by a communicative partner in appropriate social contexts. The role and impact of these receptive skills on communication and language development has often been overlooked in the assessment of an intervention. Practitioners should increase their attention to language comprehension in augmented language learning and use in order to better meet the communication needs of individuals such as our participants.

Support for Promoting Spoken Word Production and Printed Word Recognition Skills Another important direction for practice is the role of the SAL in expanding speech production and word recognition skills. SAL experience provides a unique configuration of speech, symbols, and printed words in natural conversational exchanges. Two significant byproducts for our participants of SAL experience were increases in speech production and printed English word recognition.

Frequently, practitioners and parents have expressed concerns regarding augmentation and its possible negative effect on speech development. Our findings, however, suggest that their concerns about such an effect are unfounded. The use of the SAL *facilitated* speech production. It did not inhibit or prevent speech development or use in these youth. It also provided a foundation for printed word recognition. These data provide practitioners with empirical support for the use of augmented communication systems such as the SAL. These findings also support the clinical reports of such outcomes.

Use of Systematic and Consistent Measurement Tools Another direction for practice concerns the development of innovative measurement tools. Traditional measurement tools, such as standardized tests, do not work very well when measuring functional communicative gains. We need to develop alternative ways to assess symbol learning and use.

Because SAL experience occurs in everyday settings and utilizes communicative partners as teachers, traditional discrete trial data (e.g., trials to criterion) do not always provide a valid indication of change. Our measurement tools (CUPS, VAMs, and QUESTs) provide a comprehensive approach for monitoring the communicative progress of individuals such as our participants in a variety of natural environments (i.e., home, school). These measurement tools offer easily adapted methods whereby change in communicative use, symbol knowledge, and partner perception can be documented and assessed in multiple educational and clinical settings.

REFERENCES

Adamson, L.B., Romski, M.A., Deffebach, K., & Sevcik, R.A. (1992). Symbol vocabulary and the focus of conversations: Augmenting language development for youth with mental retardation. *Journal of Speech and Hearing Research, 35,* 1333–1344.

Beukelman, D.R., & Mirenda, P. (1992). *Augmentative and alternative communication: Management of severe communication disorders in children and adults.* Baltimore: Paul H. Brookes Publishing Co.

Bonta, J. L., & Watters, R. G. (1983). Use of manual signs by developmentally disordered speech-deficient children in delayed auditory-to-picture matching to sample. *Analysis and Intervention in Developmental Disabilities, 3,* 295–309.

Bruner, J. (1983). *Child's talk.* New York: Norton.

Ehri, L., & Roberts, K. (1979). Do beginners learn printed words better in contexts or in isolation? *Child Development, 50,* 675–685.

Ellis, N.R. (1970). *International review of research in mental retardation* (Vol. 4, pp. 1–32). New York: Academic Press.

Fulwiler, R.L., & Fouts, R.S. (1976). Acquisition of American Sign Language by a non-communicating autistic child. *Journal of Autism and Childhood Schizophrenia, 6,* 43–51.

Gibson, E. (1973). Development of perception: Discrimination of depth compared with discrimination of graphic symbols. In J. Wright & J. Kagan (Eds.), *Basic cognitive processes in children* (pp. 5–23). Chicago: University of Chicago Press.

Golinkoff, R.M., Mervis, C.B., & Hirsh-Pasek, K. (1994). Early object labels: The case for lexical principles. *Journal of Child Language, 21,* 125–155.

Kent, R., Weismer, G., Kent, J., & Rosenbek, J. (1989). Toward phonetic intelligibility testing in dysarthria. *Journal of Speech and Hearing Disorders, 54*, 482–499.

Koppenhaver, D., Coleman, P., Kalman, S., & Yoder, D. (1991). The implications of emergent literacy research for children with developmental disabilities. *American Journal of Speech-Language Pathology, 1*, 38–44.

Kouri, T. (1988). Effects of simultaneous communication in a child-directed treatment approach with preschoolers with severe disabilities. *Augmentative and Alternative Communication, 4*, 222–232.

Kuntz, J., Carrier, J., & Hollis, J. (1978). A nonvocal system for teaching retarded children to read and write. In C.E. Meyers (Ed.), *Quality of life in severely and profoundly mentally retarded people: Research foundations for improvement* (pp. 145–191). (American Association on Mental Deficiency Monograph No. 3). Washington, DC: American Association on Mental Deficiency.

Mervis, C.B., & Bertrand, J. (1993). Acquisition of early object labels: The role of operating principles and input. In A.P. Kaiser & D.B. Gray (Eds.), *Communication and language intervention series: Vol. 2. Enhancing children's communication: Research foundations for intervention* (pp. 287–316). Baltimore: Paul H. Brookes Publishing Co.

Mervis, C.B., & Bertrand, J. (1994). Acquisition of the Novel Name-Nameless Category (N3C) principle. *Child Development, 63*, 1646–1662.

Middleton, H.K., Sevcik, R.A., & Morris, R.D. (1993, November). *Memory for visual-graphic symbols by youth with mental retardation.* Poster presented at the annual convention of the American Speech-Language-Hearing Association, Anaheim, CA.

Miller, A., & Miller, E. (1973). Cognitive-developmental training with elevated boards and sign language. *Journal of Autism and Childhood Schizophrenia, 3*, 65–85.

Molfese, D.M. (1989). Electrophysiological correlates of word meanings in 14-month-old human infants. *Developmental Neuropsychology, 5*, 79–103.

Molfese, D.M., Morris, R.D., & Romski, M.A. (1990). Semantic discrimination in nonspeaking youngsters with moderate or severe retardation: Electrophysiological correlates. *Brain and Language, 38*, 61–74.

Romski, M.A., Plenge, T., & Sevcik, R.A. (1988). *Intelligibility Rating Scale.* Unpublished manuscript.

Romski, M.A., & Sevcik, R.A. (1993). Language comprehension: Considerations for augmentative and alternative communication. *Augmentative and Alternative Communication, 9*(4), 281–285.

Romski, M.A., & Sevcik, R.A. (1994, March). Vocabulary acquisition patterns of youth with mental retardation using the System for Augmenting Language. In M.A. Romski (Chair), *Early vocabulary learning by persons with mental retardation.* Symposium conducted at the 27th Annual Gatlinburg Conference on Research and Theory in Mental Retardation and Developmental Disabilities, Gatlinburg, TN.

Romski, M.A., Sevcik, R.A., & Pate, J.L. (1988). The establishment of symbolic communication in persons with severe retardation. *Journal of Speech and Hearing Disorders, 53*, 94–107.

Romski, M.A., Sevcik, R.A., Robinson, B.F., Mervis, C.B., & Bertrand, J. (1996). Mapping the meanings of novel visual symbols by youth with moderate or severe mental retardation. *American Journal on Mental Retardation, 100,* 391–402.

Romski, M.A., Sevcik, R.A., Robinson, B.F., & Wilkinson, K. (1990, November). *Intelligibility and form changes in the vocalizations of augmented language learners.* Paper presented at the annual convention of the American Speech-Language-Hearing Association, Seattle, WA.

Sevcik, R.A., Romski, M.A., & Robinson, B.F. (1991, November). *Printed English word recognition by nonspeaking children with mental retardation.* Poster presented at the annual convention of the American Speech-Language-Hearing Association, Atlanta, GA.

Sidman, M. (1970). Reading and auditory-visual equivalences. *Journal of Speech and Hearing Research, 14,* 5–13.

Sidman, M., & Cresson, O. (1973). Reading and crossmodal transfer of stimulus equivalences in severe retardation. *American Journal of Mental Deficiency, 77,* 515–523.

Singh, N., & Singh, J. (1986). Reading acquisition and remediation in the mentally retarded. In N. Ellis & N. Bray (Eds.), *International review of research in mental retardation* (pp. 165–199). New York: Academic Press.

Uzgiris, I., & Hunt, J. McV. (1975). *Assessment in infancy: Ordinal scales of psychological development.* Urbana: University of Illinois Press.

Yoder, P., & Layton, T. (1988). Speech following sign language training in autistic children with minimal verbal language. *Journal of Autism and Developmental Disorders, 18,* 217–229.

Zigler, E., & Hodapp, R.M. (1986). *Understanding mental retardation.* New York: Cambridge University Press.

Chapter 7

Integrating Achievements and Outcomes

Access to the World Through the SAL

In Chapters 5 and 6, we described findings that characterized the communicative use and vocabulary mastery achievements of our participants as a group across a 2-year span of time. This series of investigations provided a detailed characterization of the language skills our participants acquired as well as a discussion of some of the factors that may have influenced specific aspects of their augmented language learning. Our findings demonstrated that youth with moderate or severe mental retardation and concomitant spoken language impairments can have significant potential for language learning through augmented means. The SAL permitted them to reveal their previously untapped capacities for using symbols in social exchange.

It is important to note that, when we observe the participants today, we see and interact with individuals who are strikingly different than they were when they began participation in the study. Chapter 3 described some of our initial impressions of our participants and noted that the participants were individuals who had had very little success with conventional forms of communication during their life experiences. At the onset of our investigation, whether or not they would become successful symbolic communicators was clearly an open question. Ultimately, they *were* successful and acquired the power that a conventional means of communication can provide. The extent of the changes in our participants was so great that it can be difficult for a present-day observer to understand why the participant may have required the System for Augmenting Language (SAL) in the first place.

As we characterize their individual accomplishments, the longitudinal nature of our investigation, highlighted in Chapter 1, needs to be reemphasized. This feature permitted us to gain a broad window on the changes in our participants' skills over time. We were able to monitor the chronology of skill development and illustrate the relationships between early developing skills, such as the acquisition of the initial symbol, and more complex skills, such as symbol combinations, which emerged later in the process. Communication is such a complex interactive process that investigators are usually able to study only specific pieces of the process, not the long-term process itself. Typically, research studies have focused on discrete aspects of communicative behavior, such as a study of requesting skills by persons with severe mental retardation. One of the challenges of a longitudinal investigation such as ours is to critically report these individual detailed pieces of the puzzle while putting the pieces together to form a comprehensive picture. Perhaps, however, the more difficult goal is to provide an adequate description of the successfully functioning individuals that we came to know.

This chapter focuses on integrating the patterns of the participants' achievements with their related outcomes in order to provide a comprehensive description of our participants. First, we examine individual participant achievement across studies and look for patterns in their performances. Second, we describe domains of change that are often elusive to quantitative measurement, such as community inclusion, family perspectives, transitions to work, and the perceptions and attitudes of others about our participants. Finally, we discuss follow-up data that illustrate the character of the participants' communications with and without their SALs and when compared with two other groups of youth with mental retardation: those who speak and those who do not speak but who have not had SAL experience.

PATTERNS OF ACHIEVEMENT

Given the many and varied domains in which we studied the participants, we were interested in determining how individual participants performed across them and if there were specific achievement patterns that emerged from the groups. We identified 10 domains across the longitudinal study in which to examine performance:

1. Communicates with adults
2. Communicates with peers
3. Produces symbol combinations
4. Comprehends initial symbol vocabulary
5. Produces initial symbol vocabulary
6. Maintains vocabulary from Year 1 to Year 2
7. Has a vocabulary greater than 35 symbols at Year 2
8. Improves speech intelligibility
9. Recognizes printed English words
10. Fast maps the meaning of novel words+symbols

We employed a dichotomous coding scheme (yes and no) and operationally defined what constituted yes and no for each domain category. We then coded each participant's achievement in every domain based on his documented performance. Table 7.1 presents the results of each participant's performance in each domain category.

Four participants (DC, JA, MH, and TE) achieved skills in every domain. Five participants (DE, EC, JL, KW, and TF) achieved skills in at least 7 of the 10 domains. They encountered difficulty with only a few domains: maintaining vocabulary across years (DE, JL, and TF), producing symbol combinations (EC, TF, and KW), improving speech intelligibility (DE and JL), and recognizing printed English words (KW). In addition, JL did not demonstrate fast mapping skills. An examination of his errors during the fast mapping comprehension assessment task, however, indicated that 63% of his errors consisted of choosing the distractor novel object that was added to the set for the assessment. This analysis suggested that he understood a portion of the rule (novelty), but had not completely worked out the entire principle.

The achievements of BB, KH, FG, and GJ in the 10 domains were much more modest. All four communicated with adults and comprehended their initial symbol vocabularies. By the end of Year 2, BB showed some recognition of printed English words, and KH produced ordered symbol combinations.

A review of the individual performance patterns in Table 7.1 suggests that at least two distinct patterns of achievement emerged from the participants' performance in the various domains (Romski & Sevcik, 1992). Nine participants (DC, DE, EC, JA, JL, KW, MH,

Table 7.1. Patterns of achievement in the 10 domain categories

	Participants												
	Home instruction group						School instruction group						
Domain	BB	DC	DE	JL	KH	TF	EC	FG	GJ	JA	KW	MH	TE
Communicates with adults	Y	Y	Y	Y	Y	Y	Y	Y	Y	Y	Y	Y	Y
Communicates with peers	N	Y	Y	Y	N	Y	Y	N	N	Y	Y	Y	Y
Produces symbol combinations	N	Y	Y	Y	Y	N	N	N	N	Y	N	Y	Y
Comprehends initial symbol vocabulary	Y	Y	Y	Y	Y	Y	Y	Y	Y	Y	Y	Y	Y
Produces initial symbol vocabulary	N	Y	Y	Y	N	Y	Y	N	N	Y	Y	Y	Y
Maintains vocabulary from Year 1 to Year 2	N	Y	N	N	N	N	Y	N	N	Y	Y	Y	Y
Has at Year 2 vocabulary > 35 symbols	N	Y	Y	Y	N	Y	Y	N	N	Y	Y	Y	Y
Improves speech intelligibility	N	Y	N	N	N	Y	Y	N	N	Y	Y	Y	Y
Recognizes printed English words	Y	Y	Y	Y	N	Y	Y^a	N	N	Y^a	N	Y^a	Y
Fast maps novel words +symbols	N	Y	Y	N	N	Y	Y	N	N	Y	Y	Y	Y

Y = Yes, N = No.
^{a} = Recognized printed English words at onset of study.

TE, and TF) evidenced what we termed an *advanced achievement pattern*, which comprised the fairly swift acquisition of symbols followed by the emergence of symbol combinations and other symbolic skills (e.g., printed word recognition). We described this pattern as *advanced* because it permitted the participants to use basic skills as a firm foundation from which to advance and to develop skills in other domains.

The other four participants (BB, FG, GJ, and KH) evidenced the second distinct pattern, which we termed a *beginning achievement pattern*. This pattern consisted of the slow acquisition of a small set (fewer than 35) of single lexigrams for comprehension and production. We termed this pattern beginning because it suggested that the participants developed a set of basic skills for effective communication from which they could build additional communication skills. Although they had not yet generalized their skills to other domains, two of these four participants were evidencing signs of new skill development.

A number of factors may have contributed to our participants' distinct patterns of achievement. The initial instructional group (home or school) in which participants were placed did not appear to contribute to the differences, because the four participants evidencing a beginning achievement pattern were equally distributed between both groups. The participants' intellectual functioning was probably not a determining factor in achievement pattern, because participants evidencing severe mental retardation were represented in both patterns. Although all the beginning achievers had a diagnosis of severe mental retardation, the advanced achievers had mixed diagnoses (moderate and severe).

The participants' performance on the battery of formal and informal language and cognitive measures administered prior to their participation in the study may help to distinguish the two patterns of achievement. Table 3.1, which described the participants' cognitive skills, suggests some variability in performance. GJ's matching and sorting skills, for example, fell well below those of all the other participants. No specific cognitive skills, however, differentiated all four beginning participants from the other participants. A description of the participants' representational abilities clearly indicates that FG's and GJ's representational abilities fell consistently below those of the remaining participants (see Table 3.2). Table 3.3 showed that the four participants with a beginning pattern did not obtain a basal score on the PPVT–R and had fairly low vocabulary comprehension scores on the ACLC (but so did TF). With respect to production, Table 3.4 showed that FG and GJ demonstrated reduced performance on the lexigram-matching task when compared with the other participants.

Influences on Achievement

In general, this review suggests that low matching and sorting, representational, and lexigram-matching skills distinguished FG and GJ from the other participants. Restricted speech comprehension skills on formal measures was a characteristic common to our four beginning achievers. Their adult communicative partners appeared to recognize this factor because they provided more augmented input than did the partners of youth with advanced achievement patterns (see Chapter 5 and Sevcik, Romski, Watkins, & Deffebach, 1995). These findings, although certainly preliminary given the small sample size, suggest that a combination of factors may contribute to individual patterns of achievement.

With our augmented language approach, the participant is not overtly taught relationships between symbols and their referents. Instead, the participant has to extend his existing learning abilities in order to make new connections that involve learning the rule that "symbols refer." If the relationship between a spoken word and its referent has been established through previous experience and then the SAL is provided, existing receptive and representational skills may serve as a foundation on which the participant can build a relationship between the visual symbols he is acquiring and his already-established understanding of spoken words. Perhaps, however, FG's and GJ's difficulty is even more basic than their inability to use speech comprehension skills as a foundation for augmented language learning. It may be that they have not established the underlying ability to form equivalence relationships in which symbols are invested with all of the characteristics of the referent (McIlvane, Dube, Green, & Serna, 1993). Our advanced achievers used the generalized rule that each symbol represents a real-world referent in order to pair the symbol with the spoken word produced when the symbol was activated on the display. Our beginning achievers, evidencing little or no speech comprehension, have less of a foundation of word understanding with which to link visual symbols and their referents. Thus, they must begin the acquisition process by establishing the relationship between a visual symbol and its referent, relying on cues in the communicative environment to extract visual symbol meaning.

Given the small number of symbols learned and the lack of generalization to other domains, our beginning achievers may have been using a different, less sophisticated learning strategy than our advanced achievers (i.e., associational versus mediational or rule-governed learning). Meador and Rumbaugh (1981) studied the relational learning abilities of seven youth with severe mental retardation who had participated in a language instructional program. They found that one of the seven participants required twice as many trials as the other six in order to learn the two-choice abstract picture discrimination task and demonstrated chance-level performance on three subsequent transfer tests where novel stimuli were introduced into the already-learned pairs of pictures. They also noted that this participant had been "removed from the language project due to a failure in progress" (p. 408). Although Meador and Rumbaugh did not detail the particular reasons for the youth's failure to progress, it is possible that this individual might have been similar to our beginning achievers. The use of different learning strategies may provide some insight into the factors that might distinguish our beginning and advanced symbol achievers.

ADDITIONAL DOMAINS OF CHANGE

In addition to the domains described above in connection with patterns of achievement, the other domains in which our participants exhibited change are more elusive to quantitative measurements including communicating in inclusive settings, transitions from school to work, family perspectives, and the perceptions and attitudes of others. Since the original 2 years of intensive data collection, we have had the opportunity to follow our participants' communication development at home, at school, and in the community. In this section, we provide examples of changes we observed and discuss their impact on our participants' ability to function in a wide range of settings.

Communicating in Inclusive Settings Using the SAL

One particularly desirable outcome of SAL experience is independent communication. Independent communication permits an individual to interact with a range of partners including those who are unfamiliar with the participant. Although familiar partners, such as parents and teachers, are likely to understand the majority of our participants' communications, unfamiliar partners, such as store clerks, are not. Because these partners do not know the participant, the participant's communication must stand on its own. If translation by a familiar partner is necessary, the participant's communicative independence is substantially compromised (Romski, Sevcik, & Joyner, 1984).

In the general community, unfamiliar partners abound. For our participants, community participation included, for example, leisure activities, eating in restaurants, shopping in stores, and attending church services. At the time of our study, community integration was a primary focus of instruction in the Clayton County school programs. As part of their educational programs, participants were involved in a number of school and community activities.

We observed increased communicative interactions with unfamiliar partners. The clerk at a fast-food restaurant, for example, could understand JA's SAL communication and take his food order message without the need for interpretation. KW was able to ask the clerk in a music store at the mall for assistance in finding a specific audiocassette he wanted by asking, "HELP TAPE," and then pointing to a photograph of the specific tape he wanted to purchase. When the tape was located, KW ended the exchange by saying, "THANK YOU." Thus, our participants could communicate with unfamiliar partners more independently with the SAL.

Transitions from School to Work

As some of the participants matured, their educational programs included transition activities. The Clayton County schools participated in Project SETS (Supported Employment and Transition Services) (Alberto, Elliott, Taber, Houser, & Andrews, 1993), a Georgia State University demonstration project that provided support to the school system for transitions from school to work. Transition services are defined as

> a coordinated set of activities for a student, designed within an outcome-oriented process, which promotes movement from school to post-school activities, including post-secondary education, vocational training, integrated employment (including supported employment), continuing education adult services, independent living, or community participation. (Individuals with Disabilities Education Act Amendments of 1991, § 602[A], 20 U.S.C. § 1401[a])

These services are implemented through the student's individualized education program (IEP) beginning no later than 16 years of age (Rusch, Szymanski, & Chadsey-Rusch, 1992).

As part of Project SETS, participants' SAL use was extended to additional settings, specifically job training sites. Their communicative abilities became particularly important as they were faced with vocational demands. Their vocabularies needed to be modified in order to facilitate their communicative effectiveness in these new situations, for example, being able to ask for "MORE SMALL HANGERS" in order to hang shirts up for display at a discount clothing store. The SAL provided these youth with a conventional way to communicate with their co-workers, to indicate a problem, or to ask for assistance. Their communicative abilities using the SAL permitted them to make their wants and needs known during job training. DE, for example, approached his job coach and used his communication device to say, "I'M FINISHED." His job coach asked him if he would like to take his break, to which DE replied,

"YES." Use of the SAL also facilitated these participants' abilities to interact with other employees on the job site, particularly during breaks. We observed the SAL foster interactions with other employees because it permitted both partners to engage in an interpretable conversation. For example, during a break, JA greeted a co-worker by saying, "HELLO." She asked him how he was, and he replied, "FINE." They sat down to have a drink and the co-worker said, "Next week we don't work." JA responded by nodding and saying, "NO WORK." Overall, then, these participants' use of the SAL for communication was absolutely necessary for success in job training and work-related situations.

Family Perspectives

Although natural settings include home as well as school and community environments, studies of augmented language learning have most often been based in school settings (e.g., Beukelman & Mirenda, 1992; Reichle, York, & Sigafoos, 1991). School provides an opportunity to examine the student's communicative skills in a setting in which activities are highly structured and group instruction is the norm. In contrast, home affords an occasion to examine the individual's communicative skills in a family setting as well as the family's use of the SAL. The findings we reported in Chapters 5 and 6 suggest that home and school were equally successful as environments for participants to learn to use the SAL for communication. The subtle differences between groups in partner input did not appear to have a differential influence on the participants' abilities to initially learn and successfully use the SAL for communication.

Including families in our study permitted us to gain a family perspective on the SAL and its fit into everyday life. When each family made the initial commitment to participate in our research project, they indicated their willingness to take a chance on an intervention that was considered experimental. When families heard that the project was getting underway, they aggressively sought us out, even though there was no guarantee that they would actually participate in this study. Without exception, each family was very giving and patient with us and with the research process. They all welcomed us into their homes and permitted us to gain unique insights into augmented language development. Without them, we would not have been able to undertake, let alone complete, this longitudinal study.

As discussed in Chapter 4, we had regular contact with our families across the 2 years of the study. We met with them as a group at the Language Research Center every other month during the school year and came to know each family. They came to us for advice and support, and we provided it as best we could. At each group meeting, we spent time discussing issues related to the project. For example, some issues that the families raised concerned transporting the Words+ system to and from school on the bus, finding convenient times to collect communicative use probes (CUPs) at home, changing vocabulary, and maintaining the Words+ system, to name a few topics. After we discussed such SAL-related issues, we ended each session with refreshments to provide a bit of time for conversation and informal exchange of information. For us, this became a time of observation as well. Parents discussed a broad range of issues. For one family, recognizing that their child might learn to read was a topic for discussion. We also observed the parents of older participants provide guidance to the parents of younger participants on issues ranging from summer sleep-away camps to group homes and trust funds.

The families were fairly diverse in background and composition as was mentioned in Chapter 3. The two oldest participants in the study, for example, were born just prior to the passage of PL 94-142 (Education for All Handicapped Children Act of 1975). These families had fought hard for their children to receive an education and thus had quite a different agenda from that of the families of our participants who were born later. Both of these older families wished that the SAL intervention had come sooner in their sons' lives. In fact, one parent was a strong proponent of including the SAL in early communication intervention programs. She felt that if her son had had the benefit of communication at a very young age, she might have had different expectations for him, and, in turn, he might have functioned differently.

One of the highlights of our interactions with our families came toward the end of the 2-year study period. We gave a presentation at the annual state Arc (formerly the Association for Retarded Citizens) meeting (Romski & Sevcik, 1986). This presentation included brief words from us and then a panel discussion with some of our parents and teachers. One question addressed to us was why we chose to use arbitrary symbols, which is a question we are often asked. One father quickly volunteered to answer this question with an example. He observed that the symbol OUTSIDE could stand for the back yard, the front yard, the sidewalk, grass, trees, or sky, for example. He explained that a photograph or line drawing would depict only one of the referents, and it might constrain his son's symbol use and his understanding of the word. In contrast, the arbitrary lexigram symbol for OUTSIDE, however, looked like none of those referents. In his opinion, then, it was a better choice for his son because the lexigram stood for the range of what outside might mean.

Both families and school personnel played integral roles in the participants' process of language learning. A longitudinal perspective offered a different view of the role of families than would have been seen if only a brief sample had been examined. As reported in Chapter 5, our findings also suggested that the long-term picture may not remain consistent. In Year 2, participants in both groups and their partners had access to the communication device at home *and* at school. There was a decline in the use of the device at home for the original home instructional group. A few parents reported that, because the device was now available at school, they did not need to be the teachers, and in a sense they seemed to have relinquished ownership of the SAL to the school and its more formal and traditional role as the place of instruction. Parents whose children began to use the SAL as part of the school group observed communication success and diligently incorporated the device into home communicative activities when given the opportunity. It became clear to us that parents must feel empowered to take on the role of partner and not feel that they must be teachers. Communication is a 24-hour-a-day process for which every communicator is responsible.

Our interactions with families gave us a new-found respect for the challenges they face every day. As researchers and practitioners, we often think that families do not do enough with respect to their children's interventions and education. In our experience, these families were always trying to do what was best for their sons. But they were juggling this in the broader perspective of their individual and collective lives, including, among other aspects, their jobs and their other children.

Perceptions and Attitudes of Others

The available literature suggests that, in general, speech and language impairments negatively affect how others perceive children and adults who have such impairments. Rice, Hadley, and Alexander (1993) reported, for example, that adults showed systematic bias toward children with limited oral communication abilities. With respect to individuals who do not speak, Gorenflo and Gorenflo (1991) reported that the use of computer-based communication devices, coupled with additional information about the individual, increased favorable attitudes of observers toward individuals using augmented communication systems. In a follow-up study, Gorenflo, Gorenflo, and Santer (1994) investigated the effects of four different voice synthesizers on the attitudes of adults toward adult AAC users. More favorable attitudes were noted when the synthetic voice was judged easier to listen to, although a voice consistent with the user's gender did not produce more favorable attitudes from the listeners. We had a similar experience with the WOLF's synthetic voice when we needed to reprogram FG's communication device to deliver a more regionally appropriate pronunciation of a word. We replaced "bulldog" with "bulldawg" because FG took his WOLF into Sanford Stadium at the University of Georgia with 80,000-plus other football faithful on fall Saturday afternoons. Blockberger, Armstrong, O'Connor, and Freeman (1993) examined the attitudes of fourth-grade children toward a nonspeaking peer who was using three different types of communication techniques. They found that a positive attitude was influenced by the children's gender, reading ability, and experience with children with disabilities. Overall, then, these studies suggest that among the factors that influence the perceptions of others about individuals with disabilities is the use of a speech-output communication device and the perceiver's individual experiences.

Although we did not explicitly measure partner perception as part of our study, we did obtain parent and teacher reports about community perceptions across the course of the study. For example, JL's mother reported that he took his communication device to church on Sunday mornings. Church members showed an interest in JL's way of communicating, and his mother reported an increase in the number of church members who communicated with him. At 19 years of age, FG used his SAL to talk with his grandmother on a weekend visit, and she told his mother that it was the "first time" she had ever communicated with her grandson. She reminded her daughter that other family members had always been present to interpret FG's communications for her. In another example, as one of our participants was independently ordering lunch with his SAL at a local fast-food restaurant, the manager remarked to us, "If your children can use computers, they must be pretty smart." He went on to say that he would seriously consider hiring them to work at his store in the future. What powerful outcomes of SAL experience—changing others' perceptions of the competencies of these individuals!

The use of the SAL enhanced not only our participants' ongoing communication with partners but also judgments of competence by familiar as well as unfamiliar observers. It is clear that the

SAL has the potential to raise expectations of competency that, in turn, influence how the youth are viewed as potential communicative partners. These increased expectations support more varied and complex communicative patterns. By extension, partner attitude change should facilitate our participants' inclusion in society as well.

COMMUNICATING WITHOUT THE SAL

One of the most striking observations we made early in the study was the degree of possessiveness most of the participants evidenced for their speech-output communication devices. Both parent and teacher reports indicated that MH, for example, cried and became very upset when his device encountered mechanical problems and had to be taken from him, albeit temporarily, for repair. JL did not want his mother to even touch his device and would push her hand away when she attempted to use it. One day at school, he was observed very deliberately carrying his original 16-pound device on its luggage cart down a flight of stairs step-by-step. Even today, JA carefully monitors the location of his WOLF and becomes extremely upset when he has forgotten it or it is in need of reprogramming or repair. These observations suggest that the participants formed an attachment to their communication devices. The SAL gave them a dimension of control over their environments because they were able to effect change through their communications. For example, DE, not wanting to miss out on an upcoming class activity, informed his speech-language pathologist when she came to work with him that she should "BE QUIET." The speech-language pathologist, pleased with the communication, honored his request and agreed to work with him later.

If the device indeed has such an important function for the participants, then what does their communication lose when they communicate without the SAL? Joined by our colleague Adamson (Romski, Sevcik, & Adamson, 1993), we addressed this issue by comparing the communication patterns of our participants with and without their communication systems.

We created an experimental condition in which our participants were offered the opportunity to communicate with responsive but unfamiliar adult partners. The unfamiliar partners followed a script that focused on the activity of making popcorn that the participants and their classmates could share. We videotaped them first when the participants had use of their SALs and then when they did not.

As in our earlier observational studies, we created language transcripts that included information about the mode of communication and whether the participant was receptive to communication. We coded the transcripts for three additional aspects of communication: whether the participant initiated a topic, whether the content of the participant's communication was appropriate to the conversation, and the focus of the participants' communications.

Given the scripted nature of the interaction, it was not surprising that our participants spent most of their time in a state of conversational engagement, regardless of whether their SALs were available for use or not. SAL use permitted them to convey more appropriate information, as well as clearer and more specific information, to an unfamiliar adult partner than they were able to convey without the SAL. Overall, then, these findings suggest that MH, JL, and JA had ample reason to be possessive of their augmented devices!

COMPARING SKILLS WITH THOSE OF OTHER YOUTH WITH MENTAL RETARDATION

Although the participants' communicative accomplishments were striking given their speech and language histories, we did not employ a traditional control group; that is, we did not follow the communicative accomplishments of a group of comparable youth who did not have SAL experience across a 2-year period of time. In our study, each participant served as his own control by comparing his performance at the onset of the study to his performance across the 2 years of the study. It can be suggested, then, that we know only that SAL experience changed the communicative accomplishments of these particular participants. We do not know how they compared with other individuals who had no SAL experience or who participated in a different intervention. Our impression was that, with extended SAL experience, our participants communicated more like individuals who speak than like nonspeakers who had no augmented communication system.

As part of this set of investigations, with our colleague Adamson (Sevcik, Romski, & Adamson, 1994, 1995), we compared the communicative skills of our participants with those of two other groups of youth with mental retardation. The first group, whom we referred to as symbol-naïve nonspeakers, consisted of nine individuals who did not speak and had no SAL experience. They were matched to nine of our participants (BB, DE, EC, FG, JA, KH, KW, TE, and TF). The second group, designated as speakers, consisted of 11 individuals with levels of mental retardation comparable to 11 of our participants (BB, DC, DE, FG, GJ, JA, JL, KW, MH, TE, and TF), but whose primary means of communication was speech.

We compared how these three groups communicated in two interactions, which differed by the type of partner with whom the individual communicated. First, we examined communication with an unfamiliar (or standard) partner using the scripted popcorn-making activity we described in the previous section. Second, we examined communication with familiar partners during two everyday activities: a mealtime and a structured task (e.g., work, academic instruction).

Comparison to Symbol-Naïve Nonspeakers

Our participants were able to convey more appropriate information, as well as clearer and more specific information, to an unfamiliar adult partner than were the matched group of symbol-naïve nonspeakers. These findings are similar to those we obtained when we (Romski, Sevcik, & Adamson, 1993) compared the communication interactions of our participants with and without their communicative devices. In everyday settings, the use of the SAL again enabled our participants to convey specific information that was appropriate to the conversation. Regardless of the type of partner, the SAL provided our participants with a better means of communication than the symbol-naïve nonspeakers had.

Comparison to Speakers

With unfamiliar partners, our participants' communications shared some patterns with the speakers in terms of their role in the interaction and appropriateness of their communications to the content of the conversation. There was, however, one important exception. Speech still gave the speakers more of an opportunity to convey sophisticated information, such as talking about absent objects and events, to an unfamiliar partner. In everyday settings, where communicative partners varied naturally, our participants functioned communicatively just like the speakers did. The differences between our participants' communicative performance during the two types of interactions suggest that the familiar partners supported our participants' communications in important ways. Clearly, these findings suggest that the impact of communicating with the SAL extended well beyond the original settings of intervention to embrace a wide range of partners, environments, and achievements.

REFERENCES

Alberto, P., Elliott, N., Taber, T., Houser, E., & Andrews, P. (1993). Vocational content for students with moderate and severe disabilities in elementary and middle grades. *Focus on Exceptional Children*, 25(9).

Beukelman, D.R., & Mirenda, P. (1992). *Augmentative and alternative communication: Management of severe communication disorders in children and adults.* Baltimore: Paul H. Brookes Publishing Co.

Blockberger, S., Armstrong, R., O'Connor, A., & Freeman, R. (1993). Children's attitudes toward a nonspeaking child using various augmentative and alternative communication techniques. *Augmentative and Alternative Communication*, 9, 243–250.

Education for All Handicapped Children Act of 1975, PL 94-142, 20 U.S.C. §§ 1400 et seq.

Gorenflo, C., & Gorenflo, D. (1991). The effects of information and augmentative communication techniques on attitudes towards nonspeaking individuals. *Journal of Speech and Hearing Research*, 34, 19–26.

Gorenflo, C., Gorenflo, D., & Santer, S. (1994). Effects of synthetic voice output on attitudes toward the augmented communicator. *Journal of Speech and Hearing Research*, 37, 64–68.

Individuals with Disabilities Education Act Amendments of 1991, PL 102-119, 20 U.S.C. §§ 1400 et seq.

McIlvane, W., Dube, W., Green, G., & Serna, R. (1993). Programming conceptual and communication skill development: A methodological stimulus-class analysis. In A.P. Kaiser & D.B. Gray (Eds.), *Communication and language intervention series: Vol. 2. Enhancing children's communication: Research foundations for intervention* (pp. 243–285). Baltimore: Paul H. Brookes Publishing Co.

Meador, D., & Rumbaugh, D. (1981). Quality of learning of severely retarded adolescents. *American Journal of Mental Deficiency*, 85, 404–409.

Reichle, J., York, J., & Sigafoos, J. (1991). *Implementing augmentative and alternative communication: Strategies for learners with severe disabilities.* Baltimore: Paul H. Brookes Publishing Co.

Rice, M., Hadley, P., & Alexander, A. (1993). Social biases toward children with speech and language impairments: A correlative causal model of language limitations. *Applied Psycholinguistics*, 14, 445–471.

Romski, M.A., & Sevcik, R.A. (1986, June). *Language intervention, micro-computers and communication.* Presentation at the annual meeting of the Georgia Association for Retarded Citizens, Atlanta.

Romski, M.A., & Sevcik, R.A. (1992). Developing augmented language in children with severe mental retardation. In S. Warren & J. Reichle (Eds.), *Communication and language intervention series: Vol. 1. Causes and effects in communication and language intervention* (pp. 113–130). Baltimore: Paul H. Brookes Publishing Co.

Romski, M.A., Sevcik, R.A., & Adamson, L.B. (1993, November). *Communication patterns of youth with and without their communication devices.* Paper presented at the annual convention of the American Speech-Language-Hearing Association, Anaheim, CA.

Romski, M.A., Sevcik, R.A., & Joyner, S. (1984). Nonspeech communication systems: Implications for language intervention with mentally retarded children. *Topics in Language Disorders, 5,* 66–81.

Rusch, F., Szymanski, E., & Chadsey-Rusch, J. (1992). The emerging field of transition services. In F. Rusch, L. DeStefano, J. Chadsey-Rusch, L. Phelps, & E. Szymanski (Eds.), *Transition from school to adult life: Models, linkages, and policy* (pp. 5–15). Sycamore, IL: Sycamore Publishing Co.

Sevcik, R.A., Romski, M.A., & Adamson, L.B. (1994, June). *Communication patterns of youth with moderate or severe mental retardation: Role of speech output communication devices.* Paper presented at the annual meeting of the American Association on Mental Retardation, New Orleans.

Sevcik, R.A., Romski, M.A., & Adamson, L.B. (1995, June). *A comparison of the everyday communications of symbol-competent, speaking, and nonspeaking youth with mental retardation.* Paper presented at the annual meeting of the American Association on Mental Retardation, San Francisco.

Sevcik, R.A., Romski, M.A., Watkins, R., & Deffebach, K. (1995). Adult partner-augmented communication input to youth with mental retardation using the System for Augmenting Language (SAL). *Journal of Speech and Hearing Research, 38,* 902–912.

Chapter 8

Translating
Research to Practice

Project FACTT

At our first meeting with the principal of an elementary school in which our research was to take place, the principal expressed quite a bit of skepticism about our project. He interrogated us about what we expected the outcomes of our work would be; how our findings would help his students; and how we would share the findings with the teachers, speech-language pathologists, and families. He informed us that other researchers had collected data in his school, and he had never obtained a meaningful piece of information from their work. He wanted to know how we as researchers would be different. We assured him that our goal was to make a difference for the students who were participating in our study. At that time, however, it was clear that we still had a long way to go to prove to him that our research would make a significant contribution to his students' lives.

This exchange illustrates the often uncomfortable relationship between research and practice. Research in areas such as mental retardation and significant communication impairments certainly has the potential to actually affect the delivery of services. All too often, even though researchers state that their findings have "implications for practice," a gap exists between research findings and their implementation in practice.

This chapter focuses on the translation of our research findings into recommended practices. We begin by discussing the perceived relationships between research and practice. Then, we focus on how directions for practice from our research were actually implemented through Project FACTT (Facilitating Augmentative Communication Through Technology), a cooperative program between Georgia State University and the Clayton County, Georgia, Public Schools.

RELATIONSHIPS BETWEEN RESEARCH AND PRACTICE

In general, relationships between research and practice have not always been clear (Kent, 1989–1990). The literature suggests that there has been a constant struggle to find a suitable balance between the roles research and practice play in the fields of communicative disorders (Kent, 1985, 1989–1990; Siegel, 1987; Siegel & Spradlin, 1985), mental retardation (Landesman & Ramey, 1989), and special education (Kaiser, 1993; Meyer & Evans, 1993). One general explanation for this lack of role definition between the two domains may be that the goals and approaches of research are quite distinct from those of practice (Kent, 1985).

A Research Perspective

Scientists contribute to the collective knowledge of a discipline. Research is based on disciplined inquiry; that is, studying something in a planned manner so that it can be replicated. Research is question-oriented, methodological, creative, replicable, self-critical, public, cumulative, self-correcting, and cyclical (Frey, Botan, Friedman, & Kreps, 1991). One important distinction for our purposes is between basic and applied research. Basic research addresses topics derived from a theoretical base in order to test and refine theory. Theory often serves as the basis for the development of specific hypotheses that the investigator sets out to measure in an objective and quantifiable way. For example, research about how great apes learn to communicate is considered basic because it contributes to our understanding of the biological bases of human language and tests theories about whether language is uniquely human. Although basic research is a few steps removed from practice, it provides a foundation for applied research. In contrast to basic research, applied research addresses issues related to solving a specific problem. Studying the efficacy of two language intervention approaches for a specific population is an example of applied research. Overall, then, both basic and applied research contribute to a discipline's knowledge base.

A Practice Perspective

Clinical and educational practice focus on the individual. The practitioners we are concerned with are responsible for providing intervention services to individuals who have severe communication disorders. Practitioners who serve the everyday needs of such individuals face an extremely challenging task: They must serve the communication needs of individuals with mental retardation who do not speak, even though there is a relatively small empirical research base on which to build interventions. They come to rely on a blend of their general training, instincts, clinical experiences, and the modest knowledge base that is available to them in order to do their jobs (Frey et al., 1991).

Practitioners often report difficulty with reading and interpreting the research literature (Ringel, Trachtman, & Prutting, 1984) because it uses scientific terms and is written in a research style. Students often tell us that research articles are dense and filled with too much detailed information about methodology and analyses, particularly statistical procedures. As a result, theory brokers have emerged to assist practitioners in interpreting existing research through the use of tutorials and application-based articles and presentations. These individuals read the research literature and interpret it for practitioners.

Our Perspective on Research and Practice

Regardless of their distinct perspectives, researchers and practitioners must communicate. As Kent (1985) pointed out, practitioners are the consumers of research knowledge. If research and practice do not communicate, the knowledge generated from research findings such as ours will not be translated into real-world outcomes. Perhaps more important, interventions will have no foundation grounded in empirical knowledge. We view the relationship between research and practice as essentially mutually informative and beneficial. Not only can research inform practice, practice can inform research as well. Successful practices firmly grounded in empirical research can influence social policy. As mentioned in earlier chapters, the parents, participants, teachers, and administrators from the Clayton County schools were instrumental to the success of our research effort. Without their ongoing input, we would not have been able to maintain the research effort. We felt a tremendous responsibility to ensure that what we had learned from the longitudinal study was shared with the participants, their families, and the professionals who served them.

TRANSLATING RESEARCH TO PRACTICE

Given the applied nature of our own research, we believe that we as researchers must share the responsibility for ensuring that the findings from our research are transmitted to practitioners, who can then implement them in practice. Given our commitment to translating research to practice, there are at least three routes by which we can accomplish this goal. The first and most traditional way is to disseminate our findings through scholarly journals and professional presentations. We have used this route by publishing our findings in scholarly journals and by giving presentations on the research findings at state, regional, national, and international conferences. Given the difficulty that practitioners often report about reading and interpreting the literature, this route has obvious limitations. A second route was espoused by Landesman and Ramey (1989). They suggested that another approach for presenting research findings is to delineate scientific principles that can then be incorporated into intervention philosophies and recommended practices. In some sense, they are talking about being theory brokers. In the concluding sections of both Chapters 5 and 6, we discussed specific directions for practice adapted from our research findings. These directions for practice are summarized in Table 8.1. But how can these directions for practice actually be used in a classroom?

In our project, we began this process by providing in-service presentations to the Clayton County school personnel and to parents about what we had learned. These in-service presentations focused on describing our findings and outlining the directions for practice. For example, we talked about why speech-output communication devices worked. In general, the professionals were extremely interested in what we had found, and those who had taken part in the study asked questions related to specific participants. They expressed a commitment to integrating the practice directions into their service delivery model. We discussed, for example, options for how the school system could increase the number of speech-output communication devices available to students, given that our findings suggested that they were an important component of the System for Augmenting Language (SAL).

The Birth of Project FACTT (Facilitating Augmentative Communication Through Technology)

At the study's conclusion, the school practitioners took responsibility for continuing the use of the SAL with the 13 participants.

Table 8.1. Directions for practice that emerged from our research

1. Language learning through augmented means can occur during natural communicative interactions between youth and their communicative partners.
2. Electronic speech-output communication devices can provide an interface between youth and the speaking world in which they live.
3. Integration of electronic speech-output communication devices in the youth's natural, existing communication repertoire facilitates a rich multimodal system for communication.
4. Speech comprehension skills can play a critical role in the augmented–language learning process for some youth.
5. The symbol lexicon plays an important role in augmented communication development.
6. Augmented input provides a model for symbol use.
7. Peers should be included as communicative partners in social interactions.
8. Augmented language learning promotes spoken word production and printed word recognition.
9. Use of consistent and systematic measurement tools permits an accurate profile of the skills of augmented language learners.
10. Augmented language learning provides youth with an entry point to related symbolic and educational skills as well as to enhanced social interactions in home, school, and community.

Part of our research team's commitment from the outset of the study was that each participant would continue to have access to the SuperWOLF he had used during the study. The school practitioners also initiated implementation of the directions for practice in schools across the county. We remained involved in order to assist in the translation of the research to practice, to monitor the continuing progress of the 13 students, and to infuse new research findings into the school program. Our research team met with the Clayton County school personnel involved with the project on a regular basis to discuss expanding the focus of our efforts to other students, increasing the use of the technology, and ensuring that new professionals in the school system were taught about the project and its findings.

SMART Exchange Award In 1989, 1 year after we began this new stage in our cooperative relationship, we received an announcement about a Southeast regional competition for Programs of Excellence in Assistive Technology sponsored by the SMART (Sharing Methods and Applications in Rehabilitation Technology) Exchange, a project funded by the National Institute on Disability and Rehabilitation Research (NIDRR). The competition provided the impetus for us to formalize our new cooperative efforts and enter the competition. Project FACTT (Facilitating Augmentative

Communication Through Technology), as it now exists, was conceived through the application for this award. The name and the acronym came from the creative suggestion of one of the Clayton County speech-language pathologists who had worked with the research project from its beginnings.

The application required us to describe the population served, the most promising elements of the program, barriers that limited success, three success stories that illustrated how assistive technology had made a difference in the quality of life of the individual served (see Appendix), and, finally, one example of how the program had adapted to change. Our application was submitted, and we were site-visited during the summer of 1989. This timing was particularly difficult for the project because school was out for the summer and only a few summer-school classes were in session and available for observation. We were very excited that our efforts were being recognized and worked hard to give the site visitors an adequate, though limited, view of the project.

In 1990, Project FACTT was named a SMART Exchange Exemplary Assistive Technology Program for the Southeastern United States. Along with the award came a modest monetary prize. Project FACTT received the award for three main reasons. First, we were a unique cooperative project involving a university research project and a local public school system. Second, we were serving a population underserved with respect to the implementation of assistive technology: individuals with mental retardation. Third, services through Project FACTT were provided in integrated settings. Our integrated service delivery model was in place before the movement toward inclusive education.

Organization of Project FACTT Project FACTT provides augmentative communication services to school-age children and youth with moderate or severe mental retardation within the Clayton County school program through the implementation of practices developed from our original research project. Project FACTT had five initial goals:

1. Integrate augmentative communication services in educational settings
2. Advance the recommended practices for augmentative communication through *research*
3. Facilitate the inclusion of children and youth with mental retardation and severe communication disabilities into home, school, and community

4. Enhance the quality of life for students and their families through the use of augmentative communication
5. Heighten community awareness about the capabilities of individuals with mental retardation and severe communication disabilities

Project FACTT consists of codirectors, one from Georgia State University (GSU) and one from the Clayton County schools, and a coordinating committee made up of approximately 10 members who represent a range of practitioners (e.g., special education coordinators, lead teachers, speech-language pathologists), members of the GSU research project, and parents. The coordinating committee meets with the codirectors on a regular basis to plan project activities and discuss issues of concern to the school practitioners and researchers.

Project FACTT's Philosophy Project FACTT's philosophy is that technology, coupled with innovative instructional strategies, can enhance the quality of a student's life by promoting increased communicative independence across a variety of environments. Project FACTT is guided by the 12 basic communication rights set forth by the National Joint Committee on the Communication Needs of Individuals with Severe Disabilities (1992), which are listed in Table 8.2. We know from experience that individual student and family needs are best met through the use of a broad interdisciplinary approach that focuses on student and family satisfaction as the criterion by which success is judged. Furthermore, the integration of basic and applied research in the context of educational settings and programs is important to achieving the goals of the project.

PROJECT FACTT IN ACTION

The primary activity of Project FACTT is serving the communication needs of students in the Clayton County Public Schools. Project FACTT services are delivered in elementary and secondary public schools, at community sites (e.g., grocery stores, recreational facilities), at vocational training sites (e.g., restaurants, motels, hospitals), and in home environments through the implementation of the student's individualized education program (IEP).

Through Project FACTT's involvement with the SMART Exchange, we expanded activities to include adopter-site education for interested school systems; instructional workshops for other

Table 8.2. Communication Bill of Rights

All persons, regardless of the extent or severity of their disabilities, have a basic right to affect, through communication, the conditions of their own existence. Beyond this general right, a number of specific communication rights should be ensured in all daily interactions and interventions involving persons who have severe disabilities. These basic communication rights are as follows:

1. The right to request desired objects, actions, events, and persons, and to express personal preferences, or feelings.

2. The right to be offered choices and alternatives.

3. The right to reject or refuse undesired objects, events, or actions, including the right to decline or reject all proffered choices.

4. The right to request, and be given, attention from, and interaction with, another person.

5. The right to request feedback or information about a state, an object, a person, or an event of interest.

6. The right to active treatment and intervention efforts to enable people with severe disabilities to communicate messages in whatever modes and as effectively and efficiently as their specific abilities will allow.

7. The right to have communicative acts acknowledged and responded to, even when the intent of these acts cannot be fulfilled by the responder.

8. The right to have access at all times to any needed augmentative and alternative communication devices and other assistive devices, and to have those devices in good working order.

9. The right to environmental contexts, interactions, and opportunities that expect and encourage persons with disabilities to participate as full communicative partners with other people, including peers.

10. The right to be informed about the people, things, and events in one's immediate environment.

11. The right to be communicated with in a manner that recognizes and acknowledges the inherent dignity of the person being addressed, including the right to be part of communication exchanges about individuals that are conducted in his or her presence.

12. The right to be communicated with in ways that are meaningful, understandable, and culturally and linguistically appropriate.

From National Joint Committee for the Communicative Needs of Persons with Severe Disabilities. (1992). Guidelines for meeting the communication needs of persons with severe disabilities. *Asha, 34(Suppl. 7)*, 1–8; reprinted by permission.

school systems in the Southeast; tours and demonstrations of our program; and presentations about FACTT at regional, national, and international conferences. Over time, the focus of Project FACTT has expanded to include *all* students who have augmentative communication needs. This expanded focus includes individuals with a wide range of disabilities (e.g., autistic disorder, physical disabilities, acquired brain injury). For example, a third-grade student with severe physical disabilities was taught to use an auditory scanning technique to access a speech-output communication device as part of Project FACTT.

Since the early 1990s, Project FACTT has enlarged its focus further to include all students whose needs may be served by the use of assistive technology in general (e.g., computer access, environmental control). Clayton County has provided support for this by creating two assistive technology specialist positions to facilitate the delivery of services through Project FACTT.

Products and Materials Since the beginning of Project FACTT, the coordinating committee has met on a regular basis throughout the school year. Project FACTT's major challenge has been maintaining an informed group of professionals and parents as well as funding the augmentative communication needs of Clayton County's students. Because of staff turnover in the Clayton County schools, in-service training activities have been a major focus of our collective efforts. In-service training has included regular workshops for county school personnel that focused on, for example, project philosophy, research findings, how to program the WOLFs, and on effective strategies for teaching communication based on the research. To assist us in keeping everyone involved in the project knowledgeable, up-to-date, and committed, we developed four products, each of which is available through Project FACTT at minimal cost.

First, we developed The WOLF Programming Manual. This manual provided a user-friendly straightforward programming guide and included a step-by-step approach for adding vocabulary to the WOLF. Project FACTT's assistive technology specialists have since updated the manual and have developed additional manuals for the other communication devices used by students in the county school system. Second, we developed a handbook that provided an organized set of written materials for dissemination to Project FACTT parents and practitioners during their in-service workshops. The *Project FACTT Handbook* is a working document, subject to revision and expansion as needed, with sections that focus on the history and philosophy of the project, implementation of the project (e.g., the WOLF, vocabulary issues, assessment, intervention and team issues), and resources about augmentative communication. The third product we developed, with financial assistance from the SMART Exchange, was a brochure that described the project to the general community, including prospective families who were moving to the county. Fourth, a 17-minute videotape, *Project FACTT: The Power of Communication,* was created to publicize the project's activities in the general community.

Supports and Policies of Project FACTT A number of supports and policies buttress Project FACTT implementation efforts. These include administrative support, family support, an integrated curriculum, researcher support, and modest financial resources.

Administrative Support From the inception of Project FACTT and throughout its growth and development, the commitment, support, and participation of Clayton County's special education administrators have been crucial to its success. The successful implementation of the project requires nontraditional service delivery systems and a commitment to a program that crosses special education labels and budget lines. The special education administrators have promoted this project by supporting 1) the funding of augmentative and alternative communication (AAC) devices by the special education department, 2) the creative scheduling of speech-language pathologists in community settings, 3) ongoing staff development and continuing education, and 4) continued research. Recognizing the benefits of this joint venture to individual students and to the field of education in general, these educational administrators have been instrumental in encouraging practitioners to implement the project in schools, homes, and the community.

Family Support Family support has also been an essential component since the onset of the research project in 1985. Because communication takes place in all environments in which the family is involved (e.g., church, childcare, camp, park), effective interactions between parents and practitioners are essential. Discussion of communication issues, parental input on vocabulary selection, plans for transporting AAC equipment to and from school, and developing and implementing communication goals on the IEP are all areas that are discussed on an ongoing basis during parent–teacher conferences. For example, as JA's communication skills advanced beyond the capacity of the WOLF, and he faced the transition from school to work, the Project FACTT team recommended that he obtain a new, more sophisticated, communication device to serve his needs. JA's mother took the recommendation and independently spearheaded the funding of his new speech-output communication device (i.e., a laptop computer with Words+ software) by petitioning local organizations to provide funds for its purchase. JA now has his own personal computer that guarantees his ability to communicate independently in the future.

An Integrated Curriculum The Syracuse curriculum (Ford et al., 1989) provides the framework for integrating communication skills into all domains of an individual's instruction in Clayton County's program. The Project FACTT Questionnaire, shown in Figure 8.1, addresses issues of communicative system use, student

Project FACTT Questionnaire

Student's name: _____ Week of: _____

Completed by: _____ Date: _____

PLEASE PLACE A MARK (X) NEXT TO THE RESPONSE(S) THAT BEST DESCRIBES YOUR EXPERIENCE DURING THE PAST WEEK.

1. How frequently did this student use the AAC system this past week?

   Daily, 5 days _____ Sometimes, 1–4 days _____

2. During which activities did this student use the AAC system this past week?

   Mealtime _____   Snacktime _____   Home living _____

   Self-help _____   Leisure/PE _____   Community _____

   OT/PT/MT _____   Cognitive/academic _____

   Other _____

3. If the AAC system was used in community settings, where was it used?

   _____

4. Did the student have an adequate vocabulary to express himself or herself during these activities? Y _____ N _____

5. Did this student initiate any communication with you this past week using the AAC system? Y _____ N _____

6. How have you used the system to communicate with this student?

   Ask a question _____   Make a request _____

   Give an instruction _____   Label an item _____

   Make a comment _____   Clarify a verbalization _____

   Answer a question _____

   Respond to the student's communication _____

   Other _____

7. How has the student used the system to communicate this week?

   Ask a question _____   Make a request _____

   Give an instruction _____   Label an item _____

   Make a comment _____   Clarify a verbalization _____

   Answer a question _____

   Respond to another's communication _____

   Other _____

8. Are there specific problems or difficulties that the student is experiencing with the AAC system? Y _____ N _____

   If yes

   Has difficulties activating touch panel _____

   Has difficulties locating target symbols _____

   Needs vocabulary modification _____

   Confuses symbols _____

   Other _____

   Please list specific suggestions for improving the student's use of the system:

   _____

   _____

Figure 8.1.   Project FACTT Questionnaire.

(continued)

Figure 8.1. *(continued)*

9. Are there specific mechanical or electronic system–related difficulties?
   Y _____   N _____
   If yes, respond below:
   System won't talk _____   Don't know how to change pages_____
   Computer says the wrong message _____
   Battery problems _____
   Other_____

10. Describe any particularly interesting communicative interaction that this student has had with you or with someone else using the AAC system this week: _____

   _____
   _____
   _____
   _____

difficulties, and technical concerns. The classroom teacher and speech-language pathologist (SLP) share the responsibility of completing the questionnaires. The results are used to monitor implementation and to facilitate communication between practitioners and families.

Researcher Support We the researchers are committed to ensuring that our research findings are translated into practice. We have continued to play an active role in Project FACTT and have served as a resource for new information about research findings, professional issues, and recommended practices. We have been involved, for example, in assessing individual students, conducting workshops, developing materials for countywide dissemination, and initiating new research efforts.

Modest Financial Resources The research project was able to fund only the research, and the Clayton County school system was able to fund only the student's education. Therefore, a very important part of the SMART Exchange Award was the modest financial stipend. This stipend supplemented the limited resources that were available to Project FACTT. These funds have been used to partially finance, for example, the production of the handbook, the brochure, and the videotape. Funds have also been used to supplement practitioners' attendance at conferences and to purchase materials for program use. We have added funds to the award by sales from the dissemination of these Project FACTT products and from donations made by our earnings from workshops and in-services about the project.

CHALLENGES TO IMPROVING PRACTICE

In the 10 years of the project, we have encountered a number of challenges to improving practice, despite effective policies and delivery of services. Factors affecting the improvement of practice include staff training, professional time, and transitions in a student's life.

Staff Training

The training of new practitioners as well as maintaining and improving the skills of experienced practitioners has been, and continues to be, our most pressing challenge. As discussed, in order to maintain and expand the program, we developed the *Project FACTT Handbook*. At the beginning of each school year, in-service instruction is provided about Project FACTT and how to implement the instructional approach in the classroom. This type of staff training, by itself, has not been enough to sustain the use of Project FACTT practices and procedures in a standardized manner in all classrooms throughout the school year. Staff development research suggests that presentations of theory or demonstrations alone have minimal impact on skill acquisition. A model for training that employs theory, demonstration, practice, and feedback results in a higher rate of skill acquisition (Joyce & Showers, 1988). Even higher rates of skill acquisition are achieved with the addition of a coaching component to the training sequence (Joyce & Showers, 1988). The provision of appropriate feedback to practitioners and the inclusion of a coaching component in the training model imply job-embedded in-service training, which requires a high level of practitioner participation in order to integrate theory and practice and thereby improve student outcomes (Orlich, 1989). Our own model has evolved to include instruction (i.e., theory and demonstration), practice, feedback, and coaching as we strive to achieve a more effective in-service system. The assistive technology specialists follow up the in-service instruction with ongoing coaching and face-to-face feedback as the practitioners implement augmented language use in the classrooms. The practitioners regularly complete Project FACTT Questionnaires (Figure 8.1, an adapted version of the QUEST presented in Figure 4.4) to monitor participation and use of the devices. Technical support is also provided by the assistive technology specialists in programming the speech-output communication devices and in the selection and maintenance of symbol vocabulary.

Professional Time

The amount of professional time required to provide AAC services can place high demands on systems and funds. Educational service delivery models and state funding agencies do not easily accommodate the amount of nondirect professional time that is needed in order to adequately provide augmented communication services. During the first few years of our program, the research project provided all of the necessary professional time as part of the study's data collection efforts for the 13 participants. Because all of Clayton County's students now participate in the effort, the responsibility of providing professional time falls on the educational system's professional staff. For example, before the addition of the two assistive technology specialists, one special education teacher and a speech-language pathologist spent more than 25 nonteaching hours preparing overlays and programming vocabulary for 10 newly purchased speech-output communication devices. Such time commitments demand the personal dedication of the professionals involved as well as strong ongoing administrative support.

Transitions

Transitional periods in a student's life are points or stages that require special consideration in order to meet the individual's specific needs. Any change in instruction or environment must be evaluated in order to provide consistency across settings. As a student moves from preschool and elementary school through middle and high school and to adult life, instructional strategies and content change drastically. In order for students to effectively communicate at each new stage, practitioners must be prepared to work collaboratively between and within each level of education to ensure that instructional approaches are consistent across settings. For example, both MH and his new teacher faced communication challenges when he was included in a fifth-grade computer class. Over time, these challenges were met through the concerted efforts of the Project FACTT team by continuously monitoring the student's and the teacher's progress. New staff members must be provided with instruction not only in the operation of the communication device but also in its complete incorporation into the curriculum. Project FACTT provides support so that practitioners for all age groups have some knowledge about how to incorporate augmented language learning into everyday communication.

PROJECT FACTT OUTCOMES AND FUTURE DIRECTIONS

There have been four broad areas of Project FACTT outcomes: student achievements, professional development, public awareness about disability, and state educational policy. First, the Clayton County students who have participated in Project FACTT have evidenced a range of communication successes that have served as the base for related achievements. These achievements range from participation in community activities to employment-related activities. In fact, when we the researchers were searching for new subjects for another study about augmented language learning, we found that Clayton County had no students who were naïve about speech-output communication devices. We had to go to other school districts to locate subjects without augmented language experience. Second, the project has provided a number of opportunities for development for practitioners and parents in the county. In addition, there is a synergy between the practitioners and the researchers that provides for the dissemination of information about Project FACTT and the development of new research questions. For example, we (Sevcik et al., 1995) published an article describing Project FACTT in the journal *Technology & Disability*. Third, through the production of the videotape, we have illustrated how innovative instructional strategies, coupled with assistive technology, can make a significant difference in the life of a child with a severe developmental disability. Public awareness about disability has been increased across Clayton County and the state of Georgia. For example, the manager of a local discount store told us that he was pleased to employ students who were using "computers" to talk. He said that they can easily work in his store, and the computer helps the students to get to know their co-workers.

Fourth, another outgrowth was the role of Project FACTT in the development of state educational policy about augmentative communication service delivery. A blueprint for the delivery of augmentative communicative services in public school systems throughout the state of Georgia was formulated by a group of educators, speech-language pathologists, and researchers from across the state and included Project FACTT's codirector. Both the philosophical perspective and the recommended practices described in the blueprint were inspired, in part, by Project FACTT's success (Hartsell & Romski, 1992, 1993). An original member of Project FACTT was chosen to direct the implementation of the blueprint, and other members of the Project FACTT coordinating committee worked on the initial development of assessment tools for the statewide project. This project has gone on to revolutionize augmentative communication service delivery throughout the state of Georgia.

Clearly, Project FACTT has moved well beyond the findings from the original research project to include all dimensions of assistive technology. The project continues to contend with the issue of practitioner instruction. Our efforts focus on meeting challenges such as changing technology, inclusive education, funding issues, infusion of research, new and more effective instructional strategies, staff development, and parent and student self-advocacy. Finally, we have come full circle: One of the toddlers from our new research project (see Chapter 9) entered Clayton County's preschool education program and became a participant in Project FACTT.

REFERENCES

Ford, A., Schnorr, R., Meyer, L., Davern, L., Black, J., & Dempsey, P. (Eds.). (1989). *The Syracuse community-referenced curriculum guide for students with moderate and severe disabilities.* Baltimore: Paul H. Brookes Publishing, Co.

Frey, L., Botan, C., Friedman, P., & Kreps, G. (1991). *Investigating communication: An introduction to research methods.* Englewood Cliffs, NJ: Prentice Hall.

Hartsell, K., & Romski, M.A. (1992, August). *Implementing a statewide AAC technical assistance program: The Georgia Model.* Poster presented at the biennial meeting of the International Society for Augmentative and Alternative Communication, Philadelphia.

Hartsell, K., & Romski, M.A. (1993, November). *Implementing a statewide AAC technical assistance program: The Georgia Model.* Poster session at the annual convention of the Speech-Language-Hearing Association, Anaheim, CA.

Joyce, B., & Showers, B. (1988). *Student achievement through staff development.* New York: Longman.

Kaiser, A. (1993). Understanding human behavior: Problems of science and practice. *Journal of The Association for Persons with Severe Handicaps, 18,* 240–242.

Kent, R.D. (1985). Science and the clinician: The practice of science and the science of practice. *Seminars in Speech and Language, 6,* 1–11.

Kent, R.D. (1989–1990). Fragmentation of clinical service and clinical science in communicative disorders. *National Student Speech-Language-Hearing Association Journal, 17,* 4–16.

Landesman, S., & Ramey, C. (1989). Developmental psychology and mental retardation: Integrating scientific principles with treatment practices. *American Psychologist, 44,* 409–415.

Meyer, L., & Evans, I. (1993). Science and practice in behavioral intervention: Meaningful outcomes, research validity, and usable knowledge. *Journal of The Association for Persons with Severe Handicaps, 18,* 224–234.

National Joint Committee for the Communicative Needs of Persons with Severe Disabilities. (1992). Guidelines for meeting the communication needs of persons with severe disabilities. *Asha, 34*(Suppl. 7), 1–8.

Orlich, D. (1989). *Staff development: Enhancing human potential.* Boston: Allyn & Bacon.

Ringel, R., Trachtman, L., & Prutting, C. (1984). The science in human communication sciences. *Asha, 26,* 33–37.

Sevcik, R.A., Romski, M.A., Collier, V., Rayfield, C., Nelson, B., Walton-Bowe, A., Jordon, D., Howell, M., & Ross, J. (1995). Project FACTT: Meeting the communication needs of children with severe developmental disabilities. *Technology & Disability, 4,* 233–241.

Siegel, G.M. (1987). The limits of science in communication disorders. *Journal of Speech and Hearing Disorders, 52,* 306– 312.

Siegel, G.M., & Spradlin, J. (1985). Therapy and research. *Journal of Speech and Hearing Disorders, 50,* 226–229.

Appendix

Three Success Stories
Drawn from Project FACTT's
Smart Exchange Application

1. TE is a 12-year-old young man with a primary diagnosis of severe mental retardation accompanied by mild cerebral palsy and significant problem behaviors. At the onset of his participation, he primarily communicated via unintelligible vocalizations and gestures. Although he had a cardboard communication system with a few pictures on it, he was not making progress toward spontaneous functional communication. Initially, our primary goal for TE was to determine if he could benefit from a high-technology device with speech output and learn to use it for spontaneous communicative interaction.

In 1985, TE began to participate in the Language Research Center's (LRC) experimental project and was provided with a speech-output communication device. The technology was modified by LRC staff to permit TE to access it via pointing to symbols on a touch-sensitive display. Prior to the introduction of the device, his family and teachers participated in a series of instructional sessions during which they learned how to operate the device and use it for communication.

TE was successful! He quickly learned to use the device to communicate a variety of messages. He has a vocabulary of more than 75 symbols that he uses singly or in combination to express greetings and basic wants and needs as well as to answer questions and interact with unfamiliar partners. After 2 years of experience with the device, TE was given an opportunity to move into a higher functioning classroom. He interacted and developed friendships with general education peers. At home, TE's behavior improved as well. His family reported increased sociability that permitted them to feel more comfortable with TE's presence in the community and made it easier to live with him on a day-to-day basis. In addition, his attention to educational tasks has increased, and his overall speech intelligibility has improved significantly so that some words are understandable by strangers. Other educational improvements are also evident. He has made a smooth transition from the elementary school to the junior high school setting and now has a sight-reading vocabulary of 25 words.

2. JA is a 13-year-old young man who has a diagnosis of moderate mental retardation with autistic-like tendencies. He has resided in foster home placements since early childhood. At the onset of his participation in the project, he was an almost completely silent young man whose only vocalizations were self-stimulatory. He primarily communicated through the use of pointing and manual signs that were not easily understood. Initially, our primary goal for JA was to determine if he could benefit from a high-technology device with speech output and learn to use it for spontaneous communicative interaction.

In 1986, JA began to participate in the Language Research Center's (LRC) experimental project and was provided with a speech-output communication device. The technology was modified by LRC staff to permit JA to access it via pointing to symbols on a touch-sensitive display. Prior to the introduction of the device, his family and teachers participated in a series of instructional sessions during which they learned how to operate the device and use it for communication.

JA was immediately successful with his device! He likes it so much that he becomes distressed when it needs repair or is otherwise unavailable. He learns and uses symbols on a trial one basis so that his vocabulary potential is almost limitless. Now he functionally combines symbols to express complex thoughts. His outgoing personality has emerged as he initiates appropriate conversations with unfamiliar as well as familiar partners. He has truly become an independent communicator. Although initially his foster mother was not particularly supportive of using technology, JA's enthusiasm and insistence that he use the device at home has resulted in an increased level of acceptance on her part.

3. AC is a 6-year-old student with moderate mental retardation who is served by the Clayton County school system in a self-

contained classroom. She exhibits a variety of disabling conditions, including a severe speech and language disorder. She communicates in single words and short phrases that are unintelligible to people in her immediate environment. All professionals working with AC agreed that determining and implementing a communication system that would permit her to express her wants and needs was the most important educational priority.

The assessment team faced a variety of challenges when determining the most appropriate communication device. The device that would be implemented had to be portable and relatively lightweight because the student is ambulatory. It was also necessary to select a device that would allow for changes in vocabulary/symbols as needed (i.e., the device must be user programmable and cannot contain a fixed vocabulary). Lastly, the device had to be relatively inexpensive because the school system was purchasing it.

After considering several different devices, the team felt that the most appropriate one was the WOLF Voice output communication aid, which is available from the Wayne County Intermediate School District. This device met all criteria established by the team. The student is able to use direct selection to access the device, so switches or additional adaptations were not needed.

Our primary goal for AC was that she would use her communication device to express a variety of language functions including expressing wants and needs, requesting activity choices, expressing greetings, and expressing physical conditions. Additionally, we wanted her to be able to express these functions in a variety of settings, including the community.

Implementation of this communication intervention has made many important changes in AC's life. Because everyone can understand the voice output of the WOLF, she is able to communicate more successfully and her frustration level has decreased. She is also more independent. She is able to request activities in the classroom and order food for herself at McDonald's without help.

In summary, TE, JA, and AC serve to exemplify the many successes we have had when augmentative communication technology has been used in conjunction with innovative instructional strategies.

Chapter 9

Toward a New Generation of Study

In this final chapter, we synthesize the old with the new. First, we look back on the participants' achievements and attempt to account for the outcomes of their experience with the System for Augmenting Language (SAL). Second, we suggest some general implications for additional mental retardation research and recommended practices. Then we look forward to the new generation of our research efforts and provide an introduction to our investigation of young children with developmental disabilities who are at significant risk for not developing spoken language.

In the Introduction of this book, we asserted that an original aim of our longitudinal study was to determine whether a speech-output communication device, coupled with a naturalistic language intervention, could facilitate the language and communication development of youth with significant mental retardation who did not speak. Indeed, the use of the SAL by school-age youth with little or no functional speech and unsuccessful language-learning histories did facilitate their language and communication development. The majority of our participants exhibited a broad range of language achievements beyond traditional (and our own) expectations. Through the use of the SAL, the youth revealed their previously untapped intrinsic abilities for symbolic communication. The unique blend of technology and natural language-learning experiences, coupled with the participants' existing skills, permitted them to learn and use augmented language without relying on repeated drill and practice. The use of the SAL actually permitted these nonspeaking youth to follow a course of language development that is more similar to that of speaking youth with mental retardation because the synthetic speech technology empowered them to speak through electronic means. The SAL enabled the youth to be perceived more as speakers than as nonspeakers and consequently enhanced social communication by allowing the youth to express messages flexibly in daily contexts and with various adult and peer social partners. Furthermore, our observations suggest that there were positive changes in the participants' overall development (e.g., knowledge base, social interaction skills). Perhaps most important, the findings were put into educational practice through the creation and implementation of Project FACTT, which we described in the previous chapter. Although we have described an intensive study of a small number of participants, the implementation of the SAL approach through Project FACTT demonstrates its generality to a wide range of school-age children and youth with mental retardation. Together, the research and the practice serve to challenge the historically pessimistic clinical expectations for youth with significant mental retardation.

ACCOUNTING FOR AUGMENTED LANGUAGE LEARNING

Given the daily conversational exchanges in which previously unsuccessful language learners now successfully and effectively use their lexicons to communicate, what strategy or mechanism can account for their language and communication achievements? In Chapter 1, we hypothesized that an interactional perspective that emphasized the contributions and interactions of both intrinsic and extrinsic factors might best provide a framework for accounting for language learning through augmented means. Our findings support this perspective. The SAL approach that is presented in this book clearly resulted in augmented language learning by all of the participants. They did not, however, all demonstrate the same levels of achievement. The range of achievements was influenced by the biological and psychological competencies that each participant brought to the task of learning language through augmented means.

The speech-output communication device, embedded in natural communicative opportunities and employed by communicative partners, permitted the individual to extract previously unobtainable, relevant language information from the environment. The specific way in which symbols were produced and paired with synthetic speech segmented the critical word/symbol from the natural stream of speech and may have facilitated the matching of the symbols with the real-world referents. As illustrated in Figure 9.1, advanced achievers who comprehended speech readily extracted the critical visual information from the environment, paired it with their extant spoken language knowledge, processed it, and comprehended and produced symbolic communications. Participants with limited comprehension abilities segmented the visual component of the signal, developed a set of visually based symbol experiences, processed the visual information, and comprehended and then produced symbol communications. Once the stage was set by the distinctive configuration of extrinsic factors (i.e., multimodal naturalistic language experiences), the ability to learn was driven by the participants themselves.

Our findings support the framework proposed by Snyder-McLean and McLean (Snyder & McLean, 1977; Snyder-McLean & McLean, 1978), which suggested that individuals with mental retardation who encountered difficulty in learning spoken language had deficits in gathering and processing linguistic information. In essence, the SAL instructional approach permitted the participants to gather and process heretofore unattainable linguistic information.

It is important to note that we were able to observe how the language-learning process unfolded and the range of achievements secured only because of the longitudinal design we employed. In particular, this design permitted us to examine the gains made by

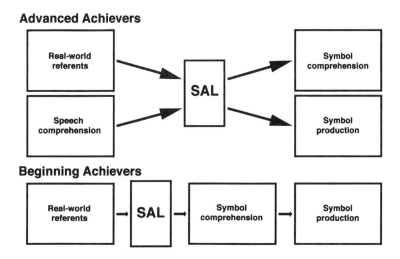

Figure 9.1. Schematic illustration of two patterns of augmented language learning.

our beginning achievers, who required considerably more time to demonstrate their symbol acquisition and use abilities than our advanced achievers.

As mentioned previously, the overarching theme in the language intervention literature has been that youth with significant mental retardation require continuous prompting and practice in order to learn language. Our findings demonstrate that initial lexical learning can occur *directly* in natural settings rather than requiring transfer from structured teaching environments. Furthermore, our findings lead us to argue that what youth with moderate or severe mental retardation need in order to learn language are relevant moments within the natural course of everyday communicative interactions. During these significant moments, the SAL enabled them to extract information about language from multiple input and output modes (i.e., visual, auditory) and allowed symbol learning to occur.

IMPLICATIONS FOR MENTAL RETARDATION RESEARCH

Because children and youth with significant mental retardation are a low-incidence population, they have not been a major focus of study for the field of mental retardation. The majority of language-related mental retardation research has focused on individuals who speak. Studies typically have used fairly sophisticated verbal tasks to probe subjects' knowledge and thus have omitted individuals who do not speak. With the development of language intervention approaches, such as the SAL, researchers can now include children and youth who do not speak in a traditional sense, but who do communicate through a speech-output communication device, in a wide range of behavioral studies. Investigations that examine word learning, attention, memory, and problem solving provide just a few examples. With advances in brain imaging techniques, studies that detail the relationships between brain structure and function and language behavior in this population are increasingly feasible. Examinations of these relationships will permit a careful assessment of the neural underpinnings to language and communication.

Much work remains in understanding the language development of this group of individuals. Investigative attention must continue to examine the contributions and interactions of a range of intrinsic (e.g., age at onset of instruction, speech comprehension, auditory skills, learning strategies) and extrinsic (e.g., instructional conditions, symbol set available, settings of use, communicative partners) factors in the development of communication and language. Both cross-sectional and longitudinal research designs must be used to examine these factors.

IMPLICATIONS FOR MENTAL RETARDATION PRACTICE

The most important implication for mental retardation practice is the recognition that communication is the key to unlocking the world for children and youth with significant mental retardation. Fundamental supports for communication must be integrated into all life activities from early in development. Our work has shown that it is completely feasible to supply such supports. Access to, and opportunity for, communication, even at the most basic level, will result in an individual's expanded participation in home, school, community, and employment activities. Undoubtedly, such participation will provide for a quality of life comparable to that available to all children and youth and an opportunity for individual self-determination.

THE PATH TO THE FUTURE

One critical yet unaddressed factor that may influence language achievement is the age of the individual when SAL experience begins. If our participants had been provided with a conventional way to communicate early in their childhoods, then perhaps their overall communicative interaction skills and adaptive behavior skills might have been more like those of children who speak. Schiefelbusch (1984, 1985) and others have speculated that if young children at significant risk for receptive and expressive language development receive augmented language experience early in the course of their development, the young child's communication skills may follow a more typical developmental route. With the aid of an augmented language system such as the SAL, symbol comprehension and production skills may emerge earlier than they would through speech alone. Having a way to communicate early in life would also facilitate social interaction and other behavioral skills that might otherwise continue to lag further behind without such experience.

Findings from the Language Research Center's (LRC's) nonhuman primate research efforts provide strong empirical support for this view. These findings suggest that early experience in which symbols are incorporated into daily communicative interactions provides an opportunity for the apes to take in information from the symbol environment without requiring them to immediately produce symbolic communications themselves (Savage-Rumbaugh, Brakke, & Hutchins, 1992; Savage-Rumbaugh, McDonald, Sevcik, Hopkins, & Rubert, 1986; Sevcik, 1989). This process resembles that of young, typically developing children as they learn to communicate via spoken language. Early experience with symbols also clearly advanced the apes' language competence beyond that of other apes who began their symbol experience at a later age.

Early Intervention

With the passage of the Education of the Handicapped Act Amendments of 1986 (PL 99-457), early intervention came into its own. Services are available to all children with disabilities between the ages of 3 and 5, and most states have initiated programs for children and their families beginning at birth. Increases in the number of children served and the need for innovative early intervention approaches have resulted in increased information on young children with disabilities and a growing body of research on early intervention (Odom & Karnes, 1988).

In a review of the general early intervention literature, Shonkoff, Hauser-Cram, Krauss, and Upshur (1992) suggested that the more significant the developmental delay, the more important it may be to initiate intervention early in childhood to ensure steady developmental progress. Although early experience with augmentative communication has been discussed in the literature (Beukelman & Mirenda, 1992; Blackstone, 1990; Goossens' & Crain, 1986a, 1986b), there is very little empirical evidence about the course of language development when intervention with speech-output communication devices is implemented at an early age. As well, the social and academic outcomes that early augmentative communication experiences might promote have not been documented.

Three factors may influence this lack of empirical data. First, in our experience, some parents of young children have been reluctant to pursue augmented communication, because they are afraid that its use will inhibit or limit the child's ability to speak. Their concerns are that augmented communication will "become a crutch" for the child and that he or she will not need to talk. Thus, they focus intervention efforts for the child solely on speech development using traditional forms of speech and language therapy, such as an emphasis on the production of speech sounds and words through, for example, imitation and practice. A second factor influencing the lack of empirical data concerns research methodology.

At such young ages, it appears to be very difficult to tease apart the effects of augmented language experience from the child's natural course of development without the use of a control group in the experimental design. The third and most important factor is that predictors (e.g., specific behaviors, profiles, etiologies) for early speech and language development in young children with signifi-cant developmental delays have not been identified. For example, what behaviors did our participants exhibit when they were 2 and 3 years old that might have differentiated them from other children who would go on to speak?

EXTENDING OUR RESEARCH
WITH THE SAL TO YOUNGER CHILDREN

The successful outcomes that we documented with school-age chil-dren, coupled with advances in nonhuman primate research and early intervention, challenged us to extend the use of the SAL to much younger children. We have expanded our research with the SAL to young children between the ages of 18 and 42 months with significant developmental disabilities who are at serious risk for not developing speech and language skills. Although the early course of language development in typical children is well documented, very little is known about the process of language and communica-tion development in young children with significant developmental delays. We wanted to both characterize and facilitate the language and communication development of these children.

A Pilot Investigation

To begin this study, we conducted a pilot investigation along with our colleague Adamson (Romski, Sevcik, & Adamson, 1992), that introduced the use of the SAL to a 4-year-old ambulatory boy with severe developmental disabilities who was at high risk for not developing speech and language. Our young participant lived at home with his parents and a 1-year-old brother. His mother had some experience with the SAL, and with us, because she had been a special education teacher with whom we had worked when we began our study.

At the onset of the pilot study, this little boy attained a Vineland Adaptive Behavior Scales (Sparrow, Balla, & Cicchetti, 1985) stand-ard score of 39. His history included significant generalized devel-opmental delays, and a seizure disorder had been diagnosed at age 8 months. He had attended an early intervention program from the time he was 1 year of age. The year prior to his participation in our study, he attended a public special needs half-day preschool program and received additional weekly private speech and language intervention. When we began our pilot study, he was attending a general education kindergarten with appropriate supports.

In the 6 months before the introduction of the SAL, he became an intentional communicator and used vocalizations, pointing gestures, and physical manipulation to make his wants and needs known. His vocal repertoire consisted mainly of vowels, though a /p/ and /m/ were beginning to emerge. Although his speech-comprehension skills were confined to understanding the labels of some familiar objects and actions in context, he was able to understand a few additional words when a manual sign prompt was employed. In preschool and private speech and language intervention, he had been given some experience with manual signs and a cardboard communication board. He attempted to produce two signs, but his limited fine motor skills made sign intelligibility difficult even for familiar partners.

We provided his parents with instruction similar to that given to families in our previous study. In coordination with this youngster's parents and based on their perceptions of his and their communication needs, we chose 34 vocabulary items that were displayed on five pages with nine symbols each. Although he had two lexigrams, we used Mayer-Johnson symbols to represent the majority of his vocabulary items because his parents were more comfortable with line drawings than with arbitrary symbols such as lexigrams. After a few months of experience, we reorganized his vocabulary to reflect activity-driven formats (e.g., bath time, reading a book). To accomplish this reorganization, we expanded his vocabulary items from 34 to 47 and reconfigured the pages on the WOLF so that each page now displayed six symbols. As a result, we added seven pages to the WOLF, and the youngster had a total of 12 six-symbol overlays. For example, symbols for GIVE ME, PAPER, CRAYONS, MUSIC, COOKIE, and FINISHED constituted one six-symbol overlay. There was some redundancy of vocabulary across overlays. For example, symbols such as MORE, FINISHED, and COOKIE appeared on multiple overlays.

Immediately, this reorganization facilitated his ability to search the overlay and find the appropriate symbol. We wanted to assess how well our previously developed data collection procedures could be applied to interactions with a young child. We collected two forms of data. First, we obtained videotaped samples of communicative interactions at home and during private speech and language intervention sessions prior to and after the introduction of the SAL. The videotapes were coded for the child's engagement states and communicative events, as well as for adult spoken and augmented language input, using our previously developed coding schemes (see Chapters 5 and 7). The codes and nonverbal and verbal events from the videotapes were then compiled into a language transcript using the Systematic Analysis of Language Transcripts (SALT) (Miller & Chapman, 1985). Second, his parents used an audiotape recorder to produce a diary record of vocabulary and communicative use at home beginning with the introduction of the SAL. The parents' diary assumed a free-form style that emphasized their perceptions of how the SAL was being integrated and used in daily interactions. For example, they commented on their child's mood, his health, and his ability to control his environment through the use of the WOLF. Although his parents were enthusiastic about maintaining the diary, it proved difficult for them to consistently produce the audiotaped record over time. They thought that the QUEST, employed in our previous study (see Table 4.3), might be appropriate for use in our study with toddlers.

When the SAL was introduced, we observed an immediate positive shift in the child's receptiveness to communication. He spent significantly more time engaged in tasks that included communicative opportunities than he had before using the SAL. Engagement state remained fairly stable during speech and language intervention sessions but increased substantially at home. These differences likely reflect the types of activities and the distinct focus of each setting. The frequency of the child's communicative attempts also increased after the SAL was introduced. For example, while his parents were reading a book to him, the child used his symbols to say, "TURN THE LIGHT OFF," when his father asked him if he was ready to read another book. The child's communicative partners integrated the use of the SAL into their verbal communications, such as in the statement "Here's your TRUCK." These communications were similar to those of our older participants and their partners (see Chapter 5).

The findings from this pilot study suggested, then, that we could readily incorporate the SAL into the typical activities of a preschooler with severe disabilities who is at high risk for not developing speech and language. We found that the SAL facilitated the young child's attention toward communicative activities and increased his contributions to communication interactions. Furthermore, we found that vocabulary selection may play an important role in early SAL success. Multiple overlays that permit vocabulary to be used within familiar routines and by adult partners must be incorporated into the intervention from its onset. Most important, from our perspective, these preliminary findings suggested that an expanded study of the use of the SAL with young children held much promise!

ANOTHER GENERATION OF STUDY

With renewed funding from the National Institutes of Health, we (again with our colleague Lauren Adamson) have begun another generation of research with children with disabilities. The aim of this study is to address the effects of early communicative symbol experience with the SAL on the communication development of young children with significant developmental disabilities who are at great risk for not developing speech and language.

We are employing a longitudinal group design in order to make comparisons between young children who receive SAL experience and children who do not. We asked parents to choose whether they wanted their child to participate in the SAL intervention. The "control group" is composed of those families who "select away" from the early SAL intervention. Although this is not a true control group in the traditional sense because we have not randomly assigned the young children to a group, we believe this approach actually may provide a stronger test of our hypothesis because these families have made the decision to focus all of their attention on teaching their children to talk through traditional speech and language intervention. We expect that the communication development of the children who receive SAL experience will exceed that of the children in the quasi-control group.

The parental response to our participant recruitment efforts was overwhelming. We sent announcements to a variety of recruitment sources (e.g., early intervention agencies, physicians) in the Atlanta metropolitan area that regularly serve toddlers with severe disabilities. We were contacted by more than 75 families who were interested in participating in the study.

The children (20 will be selected in all) are between 20 and 42 months of age with primary medical diagnoses of cerebral palsy, cerebral vascular accident (CVA), Down syndrome, failure to thrive (FTT), pervasive developmental disorder (PDD), seizure disorder, and etiology unknown. Children with a primary diagnosis of deafness or hearing impairment are not included. Each child demonstrates a significant developmental delay on the Bayley Scales of Infant Development (Bayley, 1993). As mentioned, each child is also at significant risk for not developing speech and language, which we operationally defined as children who have not begun to talk (as determined by the language items on the Bayley Scales) and who do not demonstrate behaviors that indicate they may be on the verge of talking. These children may present with a lack of vocal behavior, atypical oral-motor reflexes, significant drooling, feeding difficulties, and/or minimal speech comprehension skills.

We developed an assessment protocol that we administer to each child at the onset of participation in the study. The protocol includes

1. Descriptive information including medical history and etiology, socioeconomic status, gender, ethnicity, hearing and vision screenings, and Scales I, III, and V of the Ordinal Scales of Psychological Development (Uzgiris & Hunt, 1975)
2. The Bayley Scales of Infant Development (Bayley, 1993)
3. The Home Observation for Measurement of the Environment (HOME) (Caldwell & Bradley, 1984)
4. The Parenting Stress Index (PSI) (Abidin, 1986)
5. An adapted version of the MacArthur Communicative Development Inventory (Fenson et al., 1993)
6. The Vineland Adaptive Behavior Scales (Sparrow, Balla, & Cicchetti, 1985)
7. Comprehension measures including the Peabody Picture Vocabulary Test–Revised (Dunn & Dunn, 1981) and informal comprehension measures from the Clinical Assessment of Language Comprehension (Miller & Paul, 1995)
8. A videotaped sample of mother–child interaction

This protocol incorporates some of the measures used with the school-age youth but also includes recently developed measures appropriate for young children, specific family measures (i.e., HOME, PSI), and a measure of adaptive behavior.

The entire assessment has been completed on approximately half of the children participating thus far. To date, the majority of families have chosen to participate in the SAL intervention group, although some families have chosen to participate in the quasi-control group. For the families who have chosen the intervention, we have begun to implement the intervention using the five components of the SAL, which are detailed in Chapter 4. Parents have learned to use the SAL with their children through a series of instructional sessions at the laboratory and at home. They also have worked with us to choose a functional vocabulary for their children.

We have developed and implemented a tracking system to monitor family use of the SAL over time. This tracking system includes direct contact with the family and the completion of a standard questionnaire at 2-week intervals. In order to ensure equivalent interaction with the quasi-control group, we have developed and implemented a similar tracking system to monitor their participation in other traditional interventions. In addition, follow-up assessments of all children are conducted at 3-month intervals for 3 years and include measures of speech and symbol comprehension and production, vocal imitation skills, and mother–child interaction.

We are encouraged by the progress the children have been making. Although it is too soon to report any group-outcome data, it is important to note that the children receiving SAL experience have begun to comprehend and produce symbols. For example, one 36-month-old girl with mild cerebral palsy and other developmental delays brought the speech-output communication device to her mother and indicated that she wanted it turned on; she then used it to tell her mother that she wanted to go OUTSIDE and play.

BREAKING THE SPEECH BARRIER

It has been more than a decade since we initially conceived of the investigation described in this book. Our perspective on language development through augmented means has evolved over the course of these years so that we truly understand what Daniel Webster meant when he described the power of communication. Unquestionably, our findings clearly demonstrate that appropriate communication skills can maximize a person's full potential!

Our hope is that this research serves as a basis for challenging the traditional assumptions about language development and youth with severe cognitive disabilities. Most important, by breaking the speech barrier, we hope to facilitate the full and meaningful integration of children and youth with disabilities into our society. We look forward to reporting on the youngest generation of our research and its ongoing translation into practice.

REFERENCES

Abidin, R. (1986). *Parenting stress index: Manual* (2nd ed.). Charlottesville, VA: Pediatric Psychology Press.

Bayley, N. (1993). *Bayley Scales of Infant Development–Second Edition Manual*. San Antonio, TX: The Psychological Corp.

Beukelman, D.R., & Mirenda, P. (1992). *Augmentative and alternative communication: Management of severe communication disorders in children and adults.* Baltimore: Paul H. Brookes Publishing Co.

Blackstone, S. (1990). Early prevention of severe communication disorders. *Augmentative Communication News, 3*(1), 1–2.

Caldwell, B., & Bradley, R. (1984). *Home observation for measurement of the environment.* Unpublished manuscript, University of Arkansas at Little Rock.

Dunn, L.M., & Dunn, L.M. (1981). *Peabody Picture Vocabulary Test–Revised.* Circle Pines, MN: American Guidance Service.

Education of the Handicapped Act Amendments of 1986, PL 99-457, 20 U.S.C. §§ 1400 et seq.

Fenson, L., Dale, P., Reznick, J.S., Thal, D., Bates, E., Hartung, J., Pethick, S., & Reilly, J. (1993). *MacArthur Communicative Development Inventories (CDI).* San Diego, CA: Singular Publishing Group.

Goossens', C., & Crain, S. (1986a). *Augmentative communication assessment resource.* Wauconda, IL: Don Johnston Developmental Equipment.

Goossens', C., & Crain, S. (1986b). *Augmentative communication intervention resource.* Wauconda, IL: Don Johnston Developmental Equipment.

Miller, J., & Chapman, R. (1985). *Systematic analysis of language transcripts (SALT)* [computer program]. Madison: University of Wisconsin.

Miller, J.F., & Paul, R. (1995). *The clinical assessment of language comprehension.* Baltimore: Paul H. Brookes Publishing Co.

Odom, S.L., & Karnes, M.B. (Eds.). (1988). *Early intervention for infants and children with handicaps: An empirical base.* Baltimore: Paul H. Brookes Publishing Co.

Romski, M.A., Sevcik, R.A., & Adamson, L.B. (1992, November). *Augmentative communication development in a preschool child with severe disabilities.* Poster presented at the annual convention of the American Speech-Language-Hearing Association, San Antonio, TX.

Savage-Rumbaugh, E.S., Brakke, K.E., & Hutchins, S.S. (1992). Linguistic development: Contrasts between co-reared Pan troglodytes and Pan paniscus. In T. Nishida, W.C. McGrew, P. Marler, M. Pickford, & F.B.M. de Waal (Eds.), *Topics in primatology: Human origins* (Vol. 1, pp. 61–66). Tokyo, Japan: University of Tokyo Press.

Savage-Rumbaugh, E.S., McDonald, K., Sevcik, R.A., Hopkins, W.D., & Rubert, E. (1986). Spontaneous symbol acquisition and communicative use by pygmy chimpanzees *(Pan paniscus)*. *Journal of Experimental Psychology: General, 115*, 211–235.

Schiefelbusch, R.L. (1984). Speech, language and communication disorders of the multiply handicapped. *Folia Phoniatrica, 36*, 8–23.

Schiefelbusch, R.L. (1985). *Risk conditions for the development of speech and language.* Unpublished manuscript, University of Kansas, Lawrence.

Sevcik, R.A. (1989). *A comprehensive analysis of graphic symbol acquisition and use: Evidence from an infant bonobo (Pan paniscus).* Unpublished doctoral dissertation, Georgia State University, Atlanta.

Shonkoff, J., Hauser-Cram, P., Krauss, M., & Upshur, C. (1992). Development of infants with disabilities and their families: Implications for theory and service delivery. *Monographs of the Society for Research in Child Development, 57*(6, Serial No. 230). Chicago: University of Chicago Press.

Snyder, L., & McLean, J. (1977). Deficient acquisition strategies: A proposed conceptual framework for analyzing severe language deficiency. *American Journal of Mental Deficiency, 81,* 338–349.

Snyder-McLean, L., & McLean, J. (1978). Verbal information gathering strategies: The child's use of language to acquire language. *Journal of Speech and Hearing Disorders, 43,* 306–325.

Sparrow, S., Balla, D., & Cicchetti, D. (1985). *Vineland Adaptive Behavior Scales.* Circle Pines, MN: American Guidance Service.

Uzgiris, I., & Hunt, J.McV. (1975). *Assessment in infancy: Ordinal Scales of Psychological Development.* Urbana: University of Illinois Press.

Index